Harming And Killing Our Children

Dr. Rudy Kachmann

Published by Rudy Kachmann, M.D.

Library of Congress Control Number: 2005908291

ISBN: 1-893270-37-8

Printed in the United States of America

CONTENTS *Volume One*

Introduction: Harming and Killing our Children

Most of us love our children to the extreme. Nature designed it so. Most animals do the same.
Don't you wonder why it seems that sometimes animals do an even better job than we do?

We now know our brain chemicals—hormones, neurotransmitters, and neuropeptides—evolved to support emotions that would make this parental behavior the norm. The animals around us—cats, dogs, horses, lions, tigers, rabbits, birds, ducks, geese, etc.—take wonderful care of their children.

But we humans don't seem to have any trouble harming and killing our children.
"What do you mean?" you might say.

Our bad habits before conception of our children, for example smoking, drinking excessive alcohol, narcotics, marijuana, sugar addiction, and lack of exercise change our genetic code, and we pass those genes on to our progeny. Around 10% of our children have NAS, Neonatal Abstinence Syndrome. They're addicted to alcohol or narcotics. They have to be detoxed the day they're born.

Animals don't do that.

We are disabling and shortening the lives of our children before they even born.
Then we are not breast-feeding them long enough to give them the best chance at optimal brain development and getting them addicted to sugary foods. The group suffering from the highest rate of increase in obesity in recent years is kids aging from 2 to 6. Many have Type I or Type II diabetes by the time they're teenagers. A significant number will have a heart attack or a stroke, or even develop cancer in their 30s and 40s. Most parents have no idea whatsoever what good nutrition is.

That's why most kids are addicted to sugar, resulting in those high rates of obesity. You can buy high-fructose corn syrup soda pop, and sugar-laden foods in the schools. The schools lose federal support if they don't serve milk, which we now know it is not healthy for children.

Our government, the USDA, the NIH, Senators, and Representatives have been bribed through the lobbying of food, pharmaceutical, and fire arms companies to promote drugs, milk, sugary foods, and guns *to our kids.* It's harming and killing them.
We are promoting an "addict nation".
This book is about exposing this travesty, explaining it in an effort to do something about it.

Knowledge is everything.

Harming and Killing our Children with Cows' Milk

You may find this chapter unbelievable. Therefore, I highly recommend you get a very scientific second opinion by reading *White Wash* by Joseph Keon. It is full of scientific references and I quote from it liberally. I have read it cover-to-cover and looked at its scientific sources numerous times. Frankly, you wonder what medical providers and the government could've been thinking when they first started recommending cows' milk consumption.

Nature designed cows' milk for baby cows, nobody else. Our 5400 mammals all produce milk with different proteins, fats, and carbohydrates. A mouse for example can double in size in about a week. It takes humans a lot longer than that. Our milk does not have as much protein in it as mice's milk has, thank goodness.

I will review some of the hazards of milk, and I would be amazed if you drink cows' milk yourself or give it to your children after reading about them. If you're on the fence, I beg you to read *White Wash*.

You were constantly told that your child needs calcium. Isn't it strange that the calcium content of cows' milk is at least three times higher than a human mother's milk? The protein content of cows' milk is also three times higher than human mothers' milk. Proteins have a lot of allergies attached to them. So, it is not surprising that many children are sensitive or allergic to milk.

Dr. Walter Willett, chairman of the department of nutrition at Harvard's School of Public Health, has said, "Dairy products are the best way to get plenty of calcium." This has been a false advertisement, part of a campaign by industry and government to promote milk consumption by children.

Common Human Diseases Associated with Milk Consumption:

Growing up on the farm in Germany, I consumed a lot of cows' milk and had a big problem with acne, which continued when I lived in New York and my father's deli supplied me with a lot of milk daily. My acne became worse. When I stopped drinking milk, it cleared immediately. Acne affects at least 40 million Americans. Can you imagine how my teenage friends treated me when I always had a lot of acne on my face, including on my lips? Meanwhile, the medical community, the milk industry, and the government were supporting milk consumption at home and in the schools. Incidentally, they still do. As a matter of fact, if a school would try to promote other types of milk, like almond or soy, within a month they would stop receiving federal dollars for school lunches. I read that recently in a book and newspaper.

Americans also consume about $40 billion dollars' worth of cheese yearly. Some people think they are addicted to it. Most cheeses are 80% fat, and full of the chemicals from milk. Cheese produces a lot of obesity in children, which in turn promotes a lot of other illnesses.

Surprisingly, research has shown detectable amounts of compounds identical to the narcotic morphine in cows' milk. It has been confirmed this substance has identical chemical and biological properties to the morphine we use to treat pain.

We consume about 60 pounds of cheese per person per year in this country. At least one-third of our children are overweight, though that fraction is probably higher now. At least two-thirds of adults are overweight, with 40% obese, resulting in a lot of unnecessary diseases. Cows' milk and the products made from it, are one of the most common food allergens. Cows' milk contains at least 30 proteins that can elicit an allergic response, casein being the most common protein.

Allergies, skin rashes, ear infections, asthma, all affect milk drinkers.

The Sugar in Milk

The sugar in milk is called lactose. It's a combination of glucose and galactose many children and adults don't have the proper digestive enzyme call lactase to metabolize. This can lead to abdominal cramping, gas, nausea, bloating, and chronic diarrhea. There is a lot of difference in racial groups in having the digestive lactase enzyme. Almost 90% of Asians don't have it. Only about 50% of people with African heritage have it. Perhaps only about 40% of the white population has the lactase enzyme. So, you can see why we're having a lot of trouble. The proteins in milk punch a lot of holes in the gut and many people develop autoimmune diseases because of it.

Many of the illnesses are very serious. There are increased rates of diabetes because milk is implicated especially in Type I diabetes. This comes about when autoimmune reactions to the casin protein destroy the pancreas, which is the maker of insulin. Most pediatricians act like they don't know that. They generally recommend milk. Let's face it, allergies, ear infections, asthmatic attacks, skin rashes, acne—all common in children—could be prevented. They're harming and killing children.

Research in the journal *Lancet* comparing food intake and death from heart disease showed the highest correlation with milk. "Changes in milk-protein consumption accurately predicted changes in coronary deaths 4 to 7 years later."

Incidentally, whole milk is 48% calories as fat, 2% milk is 34% calories as fat, and, to my surprise, butter is 100% calories as fat. American cheese is 34% calories as fat.

Milk and cheese have a great deal to do with our overweightness and obesity, which in turn have a lot to do with over 30 chronic diseases and illnesses, including high rates of cancer. Cows' milk is formulated to double a calf's birth wait in 47 days and grow into an awesome 300-pound animal in just 12 months. The protein in milk does that, and we are giving it to our children.

Since 2003, the National Dairy Council has spent $200 million on its "Healthy Weight with Dairy" campaign, broadcasting the message that cows' milk helps people lose weight. We all know they know better. Is this fraud? Would you call it a criminal act? After all, that's harming and killing our children.

A subsequent study published in the journal *Obesity Research* failed to demonstrate any weight-loss benefit from dairy supplementation.

Crohn's disease, also known as ulcerative colitis, falls under the heading of chronic inflammatory bowel disease of IBD. It's characterized by inflammation and lesions in the gastrointestinal tract resulting in bloody diarrhea. It strikes people between ages 15 and 24. It is considered an autoimmune disease, in which the immune system attacks the body's own tissues. There is now some evidence that it may be related to a contaminant found in cows' milk. Certainly, if I our family member had it, I would try staying away from milk to see if it might clear up. I would also put abstinence from gluten products along with that

In recent years, it has become clear that dietary choices are important in reducing the risk for numerous forms of cancer. The evidence of fats from dairy playing a role is quite compelling. The US National Research Council stated in a landmark report *Diet, Nutrition, and Cancer*, "Of all the dietary compounds studied, the combined epidemiological and experimental evidence is most suggestive for a causal relationship between fat intake and the occurrence of cancer."

T. Colin Campbell PhD is a proponent of moderate protein consumption, with an emphasis on protein derived from plant sources, as a means of lowering cancer risk. He has studied for decades the protein from milk called casein, finding that as casein protein increases so does the likelihood of developing cancer. Campbell also found that animals exposed to cows' milk protein were more likely to develop liver cancer. His researchers were able to regulate growth of the cancer by turning it on and off by modifying the amount of milk protein in the animals.

It has been found that breast cancer probably has about a 50 to 70% relationship to being overweight. Specifically, the estrogen content is higher in people who are obese, and researchers believe it's related to that. Milk-drinking children, specifically females but also some males, who have been exposed to the excess of hormones in today's milk products, which were given to cows to increase their milk production, have higher rates of breast cancer later in life. Giving hormones to cows who are living in a cage increases milk production about 5 to 10 times. Are you getting the point? Does industry and the government really care about you and your children are consuming?

The Hormone Link

As already mentioned, bioactive hormones from cows' milk present a real problem for our children. A glass of milk contains a variety of hormones and growth factors, as many as 59, including pituitary hormones, seven hypothalamic hormones, seven steroid hormones, six thyroid hormones, and 11 different growth factors. Among these other steroid hormones estradiol, progesterone, and testosterone. These components may promote the growth of breast or prostate cancer and we should be cautious.

Also, industry farms administer an additional synthetic hormone, rBGH, and the subsequent rise in IGF -1 (insulin-like growth factor -1) levels makes the situation even more troubling. Several recent studies suggest that milk from cows who have been administered this hormone may be a risk factor for breast cancer. This hormone stimulates cell division. It's active, for instance, during the growth of breast tissue in girls during puberty. The science is not clear-cut but highly suggestive.

Denmark, Sweden, and Switzerland have the highest rates of ovarian cancer in the world, and a very high rate of milk consumption, close to the highest in the world, again raising a lot of concern. Higher rates of prostate cancer have also been found in populations that drink milk products.

You can certainly see that the promotions to encourage the drinking of milk produced by another animal—driven by medical providers, industry, and especially the government—is harming and killing our children. With the public you can see that, just like with fast food, our gun culture, and multiple addictions, it's harming and killing our children.

Our Children Are Going to Pot

We have about 25 million people who are addicted to a substance like opioids or marijuana. For about 20 million of them, it's actually the latter.

So, when we say that 80% of the people addicted to opioids started with a doctor's prescription, that's blatantly wrong. Eighty percent of them may have been on a doctor's prescription early on and became addicted for life, but marijuana was often there first. Yet, hardly anybody ever brings that up. I recently reviewed many scientific papers and at least five books about opioids and marijuana. There's no question in my mind about the role of weed.

At this time, about 9% of adults are addicted to cannabinoids, the chemicals in marijuana, about 17% of children. Twenty-four percent of smokers began in adolescence. The rate keeps on rising because of increased availability and reduced restrictions on purchases.

I have reviewed an excellent book written by William J. Bennett, who had been the drugs czar under President George H.W. Bush. Under Ronald Reagan, he had been the Head of the Department of Education. I would say being the drugs czar is great credentials. The name of the book is *Going to Pot*. I've read it about three times and check out many of his references. I used to think that physicians' prescriptions were the biggest cause of our "Addict Nation". I'm now convinced it's our rate of marijuana smoking, which starts for many in childhood.

Throughout these chapters, I will discuss the effects of the 700 chemicals that are in marijuana on the human body. It causes short-term memory loss in children and adults. Because the child's brain is still developing till about age 25, it actually causes brain damage, which has been proven by autopsies and functional MRI scans. The proof is there. Unfortunately, that's not reversible, and it makes it difficult for these children to learn and retain information. Our memories are built for taking in information, storing it, organizing it, and then expressing it in a logical form when called for. Can you imagine what that will do to the child's future, or to an adult at work?

Cannabinoids also impair motor coordination, while driving, working, at home, playing sports, or during any other activity. Falls are common. As a matter fact, a fall is the most common source of trauma for humans. The emergency room doctors told me that. In the states allowing marijuana shops, injuries and mortality from car accidents have increased significantly.

THC, the main active chemical in marijuana, causes altered judgment, increased risk of unprotected sexual behavior, causing transmission of sexual diseases and unintended pregnancies. You can see the problems that would cause. How about the effects on that child born from an addicted mother—or even a casual marijuana user?

Researchers have also found that marijuana use increases rates of paranoia and psychosis. At least 10% of psychotics have been found to be users.

The federal government has never done clinical trials on the interaction of THC and most medications people might be taking. They could potentially interact with each other, causing mortalities, accidental or intentional.

Again, long-term use leads to about a 90% addiction rate. That occurs in around 17% of people who started use in adolescence, and in 25-50% in daily users.

Long-term users have altered brain development, generally a poor educational outcome, and increased rates of dropping out of the school. The average cognitive impairment results in a decrease in IQ of about 9%. Most have diminished life satisfaction and achievement.

In long term users, and sometimes even short-term ones, researchers are also finding cardiovascular effects. Some children are having strokes and unexpected heart attacks from marijuana use. There have been increased rates of bronchitis and asthma as well. If your child is coughing all the time and you can't figure out why, keep your eyes open.

Something the promoters of marijuana use don't bring up is the great increase in potency of what they're selling now—especially in the states that have completely approved its use. Of course, unexpected complications and even deaths have occurred because of that, especially when it's first-time users visiting other states that have marijuana shops. The Colorado ski resorts for example have found that 90% of the marijuana sold there is to out-of-state residents. A significant number have never tried it before—don't you expect that some fell off the mountain when attempting to ski? I know of people who have moved to that state because of the availability of cannabinoids. What do you think? Do some bring it home? Do you think some of them might even be selling it here?

The federal government still has laws against the selling or use of marijuana. They just don't enforce the law. That's a horrible mistake. I doubt we will ever turn back the clock because of the amount of money involved. Lobbyists are bribing politicians even now. It's only going to get worse. The path to legalization usually involves so-called "medical marijuana". For thousands of years, marijuana has been used for medicinal purposes, both for the quick psychological effects and as a pain medication. In Colorado, you can get a medical card that will help to avoid most of the state taxes on marijuana, which can be as high as 27%. With the card it's only about 2.9%. The trouble is 90% of the people using the medical card say they have pain. Having been a neurosurgeon for 45 years, I can tell you about 80% of the time pain is due to stress in our life, and you can't demonstrate anything medically wrong. So, to say that you have pain, which seems real to you (but is possibly made up as a reason to get a medical card) could be the gateway to a huge fraud. Many of the products are resold and sent out-of-state. Besides, we risk harming our children with real brain damage. "What's the level of your pain from 0-10?" "Well, I'm a nine, so give me a medical card." You get the point?

When William J, Bennett was the drug czar, he was able to reduce the marijuana addiction rate to 3.9% in this country, which was a tremendous achievement, considering it's now 9% in adults. He did it through extensive education of the public.

But now a number of states, including California, Colorado, Washington (the state), and Washington DC have approved the use and sale of marijuana products. All states have experienced increased healthcare costs because of it, including increased accidents and increases in school drop-out rates. The amount of money these states have received from taxation has only been about 0.1 percent of the state budget. The healthcare costs for marijuana complications were much higher than that. So increased tax money available for the state will not happen.

National statistics reveal from the year 2006 to 2010 18% of children were smoking tobacco, while 23% where are using marijuana. Twenty-three states use medical marijuana in some form or another. It is highly regulated in the state of New York. Researchers have now found that there are 33 chemicals in marijuana that can cause cancer. Smoking marijuana, which is the most common method, causes a great deal of tar in the lungs, because filters are seldom used. Marijuana smoke also goes much deeper into the lungs because it is more acidic. Incidentally, that's why there is sugar in cigarettes. It makes the smoke more acidic so nicotine can enter the blood stream more quickly. I never met a doctor who new that. (You can find a great chapter on this topic in Gary Taub's latest book on sugar.)

Joe Califono, another health secretary at the federal level, wrote a book called *How to Raise a Drug-Free Kid.* I recommend you read it. He states children who use marijuana have a decrease in the cannabinoid receptors in the brain, and therefore have to increase the dose to get the high they're looking for. That's called tolerance, which occurs in all drug users. You see it even in people who use a lot of sugar in their food, which partly accounts for the obesity epidemic. When I tell a child that smoking marijuana may give them a pot belly, and that the girls (or boys) might not look at them, much less talk to them, they seem to pay more attention. Don't you wonder why they call it a "pot" belly?

The marijuana shops in Colorado provide customers with many different products, from candy bars, food, inhalers, reefers, etc. The main difference is in THC content. Some products go as high as 37%. Can you imagine what that might do to some people?

Let's face it, we're engaging in public policy malpractice with THC, a drug that was never properly tested by the FDA. We even have a "Grass Law," for goods generally regarded as safe. Certainly marijuana would not qualify because of its many harmful effects. We are harming and killing our children and many adults. If the child is not addicted by age 21, the addiction rate is much less, although a lot of the side effects certainly continue: the pot bellies, the increased rates of about 20 chronic diseases, including Type II Diabetes, increase accidents, lack of ambition, etc.

The nation of Uruguay is the only other country that has allowed complete legalization. Even in the Netherlands where they have coffee shops where they sell a certain amount, it is not totally legal. What they have instead is tolerance of it. A lot of people come from other countries to buy it. As you would expect, they've had complications because of it. They now have four children's rehab centers for marijuana addiction. They are regretting what they did.

When they try to legalize marijuana in your state, they will say there is an absolute need for medical marijuana. It's a complete myth. The definition of pain is wrong. Eighty percent of the people with pain, you can tell why they hurt. To give them a quick fix like opioids for marijuana will result in addiction in a large percentage cases. I know because as a neurosurgeon I lived in that world for decades, resulting in my writing three books on chronic pain. They are on Amazon. One has the title, *We Need a New Definition for Pain.*

In Arizona, 34,000 people use medical marijuana, and 90% say it's for pain. Pretty soon we will have a nation of pain people, with very few working, and with everyone using the medical marijuana card every day of the week. Can you imagine the effect on our children? Incidentally, one-third of the children get their marijuana from other people's prescriptions.

In Colorado, 7.7% of the children use marijuana. Nationally, it's about 7% starting by the 12th grade. About 31.2% of people in Colorado use marijuana, higher than the 22% in the US generally. About 3000 traffic deaths occur from marijuana in the US every year. It is especially lethal when marijuana is mixed with alcohol.

In Denver, there are now more marijuana shops than Starbucks. In Los Angeles, the capital of homelessness, there are more marijuana shops than Starbucks and McDonalds combined. Incidentally, one dollar spent on teaching prevention saves generally about $10 on treatment cost.

Sanjay Gupta of CNN, who says he's a doctor, keeps on repeating anecdotal evidence on the benefits of medical marijuana. I saw his show again last Sunday and I'm very disappointed. I think he could've provided all of us with the scientific evidence of marijuana use and saved many lives. The anecdotes he brings up are not a scientific study. He is promoting the use of marijuana instead of explaining the science to the general public. He will end up harming and killing a lot of children and adults as a result of his tainted information. I would like to ask him if he is receiving some reimbursement from the industry?

The big marijuana companies depend on 20% of the population who uses. So they need to create a lot of addicts to make their money. When these companies and legislators try to introduce marijuana to your state, they will not bring the facts because children and adults don't matter to them. They'll be speaking about medical marijuana and its unproven benefits. So watch out and get out and vote. Falsehoods and fake news will be spread by interest groups. The political debates are about the same on the Republican and Democratic side. They all like the lobbying money.

They will falsely promote the tax benefits that have already accrued, which are non-existent. The medical calls will outpace the tax money. Legalization will cost society money, and result in injuries and deaths. Incidentally, casual use also affects the brain and the affects cannot be reversed. The science of the effects of marijuana are evolving further every day and the information is never good.

I can statistically proof that a heavy drug user started with marijuana, not opioids, 80% of the time. But what also concerns me is that the stigmatization of marijuana use is leaving us. I think CNN, by using Dr. Sanjay Gupta in their marijuana documentaries, has a lot to do with that.

We need national leadership on this issue. I'm not even thinking parties. Let's face it, the Obama administration did nothing to stop it and even helped promote it with a casual attitude toward marijuana use. We still don't have a drug czar in this country.

President Trump tried to appoint Senator Marino from Pennsylvania to the position, only to withdraw his nomination after an edition of 60 Minutes in January. The Senator had passed a law by consensus (no active vote) preventing the FDA from testing Class-1 drugs, including THC. What a scam!

I even applied for the job, having written three books on opioids. I think at least I would have the passion for it. I sent my books to our governor, to Congressman Jim Banks, and the former governor of Indiana who is now Vice President.

What can I say? I'm trying.

Harming and Killing Our Children with Fast Food

Fast food means you can eat it fast, get it fast, and gather it into your fat cells fast, without much effort.

The food itself that is sold is full of sugar and bad Omega six fats, the main cause of children being overweight, obese, and having many chronic diseases, including: diabetes, memory loss, brain damage, thyroid disease, bad teeth, liver and kidney disease, generalized vascular disease including heart attacks and amputations, bowel and skin disease, and on and on. All that could be prevented by eating nutrient-dense food instead. Besides, fast food is highly addictive.

The health effects of regularly consuming fast food maybe even more severe than smoking.

Fast food is served at commercial chain restaurants, where processed meats, pizza, burgers, French fries, pretzels, soft drinks, and rich desserts are made in an assembly line process, flavored with chemical sprays and commercial ingredients that are duplicated and dispensed all over the world, repeating the same pattern as the obesity epidemic in the US. These foods also include man-made chemicals, processed grains (grains with the nutrients removed), sugar, salt, all doused in oil with minimal nutrient content. Remember good food is full of vitamins, minerals, and phytochemicals, which fuel the machinery of the body and lead to great health.

Some people call them “fake” foods: frozen waffles, deli sandwiches, frozen pizza, bags of chips—sure these are all easily available at our local supermarkets and convenience stores. But processing foods removes and destroys their fragile micronutrients and phytochemicals, which we need for cellular factories. These foods also put a lot of toxins in our body, forcing our already overworked livers to save our lives.

Toxins added to fast food and processed foods include artificial colors, artificial flavors, preservatives, pesticides, anti-foaming agents, emulsifiers, stabilizes, and thickeners. These ingredients give foods that texture and consistency that consumers expect. You can see how fast foods are full of toxins: they accelerate death with these added toxins, but also by supplying concentrated calories without fiber and micronutrients, which we need to have a healthy body.

Fast food is sold in every conceivable way: gas stations, commercial outlets, supermarkets, restaurants, airplanes—just plain everywhere, and soon Amazon will even deliver it to your door.

These foods behave like a drug that damages the whole body of children, especially the brain.

We are causing our children to commit suicide on the installment plan, making a payment every day. Some school lunches and soda machines are making a payment to poor health every day. I know of some hospitals that even have donut shops and soda pop machines in them.

Fat on the body is not just a cosmetic issue; it's better than a blood test. A pot belly indicates prediabetes or diabetes 95% of the time. Many have never been tested, or have been incorrectly tested, to make a diagnosis that could lead to treatment.

A person who eats fried foods, fast food, and processed foods has at least 10 times the heart attack risk of someone who eats reasonably healthy food. Past scientific studies, survey studies, and clinical evidence, all show a person eating a nutrient-dense diet has at least a hundredfold less risk of developing prediabetes and diabetes than one eating a diet of salt, fat, and sugar. Many parents addict their children to sugar because of lack of knowledge.

Eating fast food to or three times per week increases the risk of dying from coronary artery disease more than 50%. But the greatest risk was found in the subjects who ate fast food four or more times weekly. The risk of dying from corner heart disease rose 80% under those conditions. Eating fast food just once a week increases heart risk by 20%. It's all scientifically proven. Just read *Fast Food Genocide* by Dr. Joel Fuhrman for scientific references.

Fast food is digested and absorbed rapidly. It contains multiple synthetic ingredients. It is calorie-dense. It doesn't have the necessary vitamins, minerals, and phytochemicals for good health. It is highly flavored and addictive, and it contains excess salt and sugar.

The faster food enters the bloodstream, the higher the release of fat storage hormones and the greater the increase in dopamine, the “quick fix” neuropeptide of addiction. Because of the hormonal effects, fast foods initiate and perpetuate food addiction and cravings. The chief fat storage hormone is insulin, which increases because of sugar and leads to fat storage, weight gain, cellular degradation, and eventually cancer, dementia, and chronic inflammation in the whole body.

Addicting Children to Fast Food

Fast food rewires the circuitry of the brain's quick fix chemicals dopamine and serotonin, activating the contentment center, just like narcotics, alcohol, and cigarettes do.

Sugar, salt, some fats, and artificial flavorings have addictive properties. Eating a little, just like smoking one cigarette, can lead to a lifetime of bad food habits. Many parents, as well as the food industry and the government, are participating in this by promoting sugary foods and supporting their prices. Overeating and substance abuse share important common characteristics, including the development of dependency and tolerance—the path to addiction.

The "bliss point" of sugar, salt and fat has been well worked out by the industry. When the government said to eat carbohydrates—sugar—instead of fat, the food industry quickly figured out the bliss point of sugar. Children tolerate sugar more than adults, and we can addict them quicker; indeed, that's what's being done. Over time, these kids crave more and more sugar, but the sugar in natural foods like berries no longer have any appeal. Children raised on fast food, soda, and frequent junk food treats tend not to like fruits and vegetables. It is because their taste buds and their brains' addictive circuitry have been changed.

Fast food also prevents you from taking in nutrients, the phytochemicals, vitamins, and minerals that we all need to be healthy.

Giving kids soda, donuts, and other junk food is practically the same as handing them a cigarette, a joint, or a shot of whiskey. It hits the same dopamine and serotonin circuitry in the brain, giving them a quick fix. Unfortunately, there is just a small degree of difference between one addictive and dangerous substance and another. The same brain centers as stimulated by cocaine, narcotics, and super-sweetened fatty foods. Some people think sugar is more addictive than cocaine.

The brain's dopamine reward system was a survival advantage thousands of years ago when food was not regularly available. Nature designed this system so animals and humans could even become fat, because they might not eat again for a month. Unfortunately, we still have that fat storage circuitry. However, today's processed

Franken-food environment is killing us and especially our children, with the help of industry, parents who lack knowledge, and governmental agencies collecting money from politicians and lobbyists.

When someone abuses a substance, whether it's alcohol, drugs, or addictive food, that person's brain reduces the number of dopamine D2 receptors, resulting in a diminished reward response and a higher tolerance of the substance. For example, frequent consumption of ice cream has been shown to reduce the reward response. That means over time the same amounts of ice cream no longer satisfies the craving, and the consumption of more sweetened calories is needed to elicit the same amount of pleasure. The more fast food people eat, the more they lose dopamine receptor function.

Sometimes I'm brought to tears when I'm go to a fast food restaurant to get coffee and see what parents are feeding to their children. A lot of other parents are clearly overweight, and I see the future of the whole family unfolding before my mind's eye. I have to restrain myself to keep from saying something.
But harming and killing our children is something I am not willing to passively accept.

The Sugar Kiss

High-fructose corn syrup (HFCS), the ultimate Franken-food, is added in high amounts to essentially all processed foods. It is sweeter than regular sugar, less expensive than regular sugar, and keeps the food from rotting. The government supports the price through Federal subsidies for corn. And it happens to be highly addictive.

HFCS is also hidden and pizza crust, tomato sauce, salad dressings, and even in that shop meet used for hamburgers.

Of course, the food industry uses HFCS because it costs less, the profits are bigger, and it's more addictive because it's a lot sweeter. Food companies have done a lot of testing to determine the perfect "bliss point," the ideal balance of chemicals added to foods to make them as addictive as possible. Remember, the bliss point for children is higher than it is for us adults. They tolerate high sugar content significantly more. The fructose which is 55% of fructose corn syrup is highly soluble and does not crystallize, so it can remain effective in processed foods forever and not cause the food to harden. It doesn't rot readily either.
Unfortunately, the human cost is increased obesity, diabetes, any chronic disease. That could shorten the life of children by 25 years, and have them living with 30 years of some disability. That has been well-studied and is proven scientifically.

There is also an accompanying increase in the rates of cancer for our children and for people who regularly eat fast food and processed foods. They can be exposed to the equivalent of 100 tea spoons of sugar a day or more. One large soft drink or milkshake alone may contain the equivalent of 50 teaspoons of sugar.

For over 55 years, the soft drink industry and the sugar industry have provided millions of dollars of funding to academic and governmental researchers to influence and cover up the health risks associated with consuming sugar. This is well documented in many books. An article published in *JAMA Internal Medicine* and reported on in *The New York Times* revealed that the past five decades of research into the role of nutrition and heart disease, including many of today's dietary recommendations, have been largely shaped by the financial influence of the sugar industry. "These companies have been able to derail the discussion about sugar for decades," said a professor of medicine at the University of California, San Francisco, who was one of the *JAMA* paper's co-authors. Information regarding the dangers of modern processed foods is effectively suppressed by powerful economic interests, and they spend lots of money to influence public perception. This is harming and killing our children, and we need to step up to bat and do something about it, because it's doubtful the government or medical industry will lead the way.

Consuming fructose, which is 50% of sugar, raises insulin secretion, so consuming concentrated fructose in foods containing high-fructose corn syrup, such as soft drinks, baked goods, breakfast bars, and snack foods, can be dangerous. That's because the insulin is taken up by muscle cells and gets used up quickly all over the body, while the fructose goes right to the liver and triggers the production of fats such as triglycerides and cholesterol. We know that causes insulin resistance, a cause of diabetes with its multitude of chronic diseases (which unfortunately even occur in very young children). Insulin resistance causes fat in the liver, and a lot of damage. It is estimated that we have 70 million people with a "fatty liver" in America. The liver was not designed to metabolize the large quantities of fructose found in artificial commercial foods. Liver transplants will be becoming extremely common in the nation. That causes a lot of disability and the cost is tremendous. A good 90% of that could be avoided through proper wellness education for our parents and children.

The explosion in the occurrence of obesity and Type II Diabetes in the past 50 years was probably caused by the high exposure to sugar and high focus corn syrup in fast foods and soft drinks. Exposure to high-fructose corn syrup has created a nation of metabolically challenged individuals who are overweight, diabetic, or pre-diabetic, and have high levels of cholesterol and triglycerides. This is called Metabolic Syndrome, which has led to a health crisis of unprecedented proportions in our children and adults. The good news is that this problem is essentially avoidable by eating nutrient-dense or "slow" food—slow because it takes longer to metabolize.

The health damaging effects of HFCS can include obesity, high blood pressure, diabetes, blindness, liver disease, kidney disease, premature aging, high triglycerides, high cholesterol, heart attack, dementia, strokes, and increased rates of cancer. This is what we are doing to our children, as well as ourselves.

This collection of risks of high-fructose corn syrup also includes Advanced Glycation Products, chemical colorings, and nutrient deficiency. Because of these, fast food can result in accumulated toxic burden, resulting in "brain fog." This can lead to difficulty concentrating, the loss of a full work day, and loss of memory, and it may eventually lead to dementia. It has now been scientifically proven that a great deal of Alzheimer's disease is actually dementia related to insulin resistance. About 75% of supposed Alzheimer's disease is actually from insulin resistance. The good news is that a majority of that could be avoided by proper lifestyle. We don't need to look for a drug to avoid most of our dementia problems. This will come as a disappointment to companies like Eli Lilly, which was recently reported to have spent $1 billion on research into the cure for Alzheimer's disease, research that came up with nothing. That was not a surprise to me.

Processed foods are also linked to the incidence of strokes, causing them to occur at younger and younger ages. That has sparked an entire industry of healthcare facilities that cater to impaired young people who have destroyed large sections of their brains with fast food. The incidence of strokes before the age of 45 is five times higher in black populations, likely due to their increased consumption of fast food. Blacks are more sensitive to sugar because of the genetic changes brought on during slavery. Slaves had to eat sugarcane to stay alive; it's in their DNA to seek sugary foods to feel good.

The combined effect of fast food and processed food industries has been an explosive epidemic of obesity and diabetes, with kidney failure, limb amputations, and heart problems (especially among the African American population). Their rate of kidney failure is four times higher than the rate in the white population. (I've spent a lot of time teaching about preventing, stopping, and reversing Type II Diabetes for black churches. If you check my Facebook pages, you will see some great photos from some of these events.)

Frying Our Children's Brains with Fast Food

We frankly don't get it. Fast food affects the development of children's brains, their intelligence, and their behavior. Most people mistakenly think that your child's intelligence is completely determined at birth. Actually, only about 5% of their DNA and genetics has been expressed at that time. I will discuss that further in a chapter about the emerging science called epigenetics. So that's good and bad news, good because the right health habits can lead to a great brain and, bad because the wrong foods can damage the brain.

Available evidence suggests that brain function and human potential are determined by external factors, like those on American dinner plates," Dr. Joel Fuhrman says in his great book *Fast Food Genocide*.

Fuhrman also states that there is some evidence that there are increased rates of criminality in areas where healthy food is unavailable. Can it be, in addition to obvious and complex variables like social factors, that unhealthy food is a major contributor to the increased rates of disease, lower achievement, and increased rates of criminality?

Early in life, the brain is highly dependent on nutrients, vitamins, minerals, and phytochemicals, and it can be significantly impaired by poor nutrition. Many school lunch programs provide sugary drinks, sugary foods, and bad Omega six fats. Is it any wonder so many of our children are in poor health? About 40% of our children are overweight and many are frankly obese.

Can you imagine how many overweight children are bullied by their classmates? Scientific evidence indicates that your emotional well-being, willpower, determination, work ethic, patience, concentration, creative memory, and intelligence all depend on exposure to sufficient nutrients and healthy food throughout your life, especially when you're young and developing. It is impossible to have normal brain function and a healthy emotional life when the majority of your food calories come from fast food.

Fast foods and processed foods simply do not contain the diverse array of nutrients that the body and brain desperately need. Yet the majority of Americans today get more than a half of their calories from fast food and processed food.

Most Americans get less than 5% of their calories from colorful produce. The combination of insufficient micronutrients and phytochemicals, imbalances in fatty acids, and exposure to fast food-derived toxins damages not just our bodies, but our fragile, nutrient-demanding brains.

Modern fast foods are specifically designed to deceive the human metabolism by limiting those outward symptoms. Commercial foods are fortified with vitamins and enriched just enough to keep us from displaying—or dying from—an acute deficiency, but they do not have the vast array of nutrients and phytochemicals that are needed to enable our brains to develop and function normally.

Chronic anger, chronic mild depression, and mental inflexibility are symptoms of subclinical nutritional deficiencies that are extremely common and difficult to diagnose.

Natural food such as green vegetables, seeds, berries, and mushrooms contain thousands of nutrients that fuel human health. We need a diverse spectrum of anti-oxidants and phytochemicals to enable ourselves to function normally. Our brains cannot function normally with a continual and unrelenting buildup of free radicals, all the metabolic waste and toxic irritants that arise from consuming processed foods. These metabolic waste toxins produced by our body would normally be removed if our nutrient exposure were adequate.

A healthy and happy brain requires a steady stream of vitamins, minerals, and phytochemical plant compounds, ingredients that are missing from modern commercial foods. Many school lunches are even harmful to our children's brains. I've been there to witness the problem.

Phytochemicals are caloric compounds present in plants that have health-promoting and disease-preventing properties. They are not vitamins and minerals, but they augment and sustain human self-function and support the immune system. They act as fuel for the cell-repair processes in human DNA; therefore, they have powerful anticancer effects also. There are more than 8000 known phytochemicals. Some other well-known phytochemicals are lycopene in tomatoes, isoflavones in soy, and flavonoids in fruits. They generally present as the colorful part of your vegetables and fruits. As a natural part of the human diet, they are necessary for cell signaling pathways within the brain, so the presence or absence of phytochemicals affects brain development, brain function, and brain pathology.

Our children are consuming an extravagantly high-calorie, no-nutrient diet which stresses the brain with metabolic wastes while systematically depriving it of all the micronutrients necessary to self-cleanse and undo the damage. A healthy and happy brain requires a steady stream of vitamins, minerals and phytochemical plant compounds, the ingredients that are missing from modern commercial foods. We are harming and killing our children, as well as ourselves.

As many as one in eight adolescents are diagnosed as clinically depressed, and many more have mild forms of mood disorders and learning difficulties. Clinical depression is the top cause of disability for children ages 5 and older.

An unhealthy diet is a major cause of depression. Feeling down every day is no fun. A significant number of children commit suicide (which is a lot easier to do when there are guns in the home). A 2015 study showed a dose-dependent relationship between high-glycemic-load foods, white flour, and sweetening agents, and depression. So it has been scientifically proven. The references are in Dr. Joel Fuhrman's book *Fast Food Genocide*.

In healthy young people, a brain imaging study has demonstrated that the ability to process emotion is compromised by elevated blood glucose levels, which are commonly found in fast food.

Excess sugar impairs both cognitive skills and self-control. The mixture of sugar, salt, and oil interferes with the body's ability to control calorie intake or be satisfied with normal amounts of food. Fast foods turn humans into eating machines, individuals with no caloric turn-off switch. This lack of self-control over eating food is like turning on an obesity-driving switch that leads to diabetes and other diseases. Elevated blood sugar levels harm blood vessels, and blood vessel damage is a major cause of vascular complications and diabetes. Unannounced heart attacks in young people are common. Fifty percent of those who experience heart attacks at a young age grab their chest and die without a warning.

One study found an increase in behavior and attention problems in five-year-olds with increased consumption of soda. This was based on a scientific study. Any sugar added to a food is dangerous. We can avoid these dangers by satisfying our sweet tooth with fresh fruit instead of refined sugars. You can make delicious desserts with fruit, and even treats such as brownies and ice cream. Throw in some nuts and dried fruits that are only a little less sweet than conventional desserts and you have a snack that's healthy for you.

The health benefits of nuts and seeds disappear when the nuts and seeds are processed and reduced to oils, which changes them into an obesity-promoting food. The increase in worldwide consumption of high omega 6 oils over the past century is a large uncontrolled experiment that is showing increased social burdens like aggression, depression, and cardiovascular mortality.

The danger of all this oil is most evident in the southern US, where oil consumption and fried foods are at their worst. People in this region regularly eat a traditional "Southern Diet" that is known for its many deep fried foods, such as fried chicken, processed meats, light bacon and ham, sugary beverages, biscuits and gravy. With this diet, Southerners have achieved the highest rates of stroke and heart disease in the world. This is especially manifested in their children. I attended a church service in the south, and frankly I could barely stand what I was seeing in both the children and the adults. Scientific research has clearly shown that on average Southerners live twenty-five years less, while experiencing 35 years of disability, including liver transplants, kidney transplants, extremity amputations, and increased rates of cancer, along with many other chronic diseases. The majority of these can be completely avoided by proper lifestyle and eating nutrient-dense food—not a diet of fast food.

Eating the wrong food leads to lower intelligence, poor school performance, aggression and hostility, depression and some suicides, as well as brain shrinkage and dementia. They may call it Alzheimer's Disease, but it's actually dementia related to Type II Diabetes. This is scientifically well proven.

What you put on your fingers or forks, and how much you move, largely determine your future.

The University of Bristol demonstrated that the micronutrient content of a diet plays a vital role in the development of childhood intelligence. That UK study started in the early 1900s, when more than 14,000 pregnant women were examined, followed by the long-term outcomes of their offspring. Researchers found that intelligence, measured by IQ tests, is definitely affected by the quality of the diet. Toddlers in the study who consumed a healthier diet had high IQs by 8.5 years of age. Those who ate more junk food and less fresh fruits and vegetables also had more behavioral problems at age 8. The fact that early childhood nutrition can have lifelong consequences points to a new opportunity to affect the expression of genes that govern brain development.

A Large Brain for Our Child: The importance of Mother's Milk

We consume bad fats, including omega-6, saturated fats, and trans fats when we eat fast food and most meats.

Our three-pound brain, meanwhile, is made largely from omega-3 fats, which form part of the membrane of every brain cell. Mother's milk is filled with these omega-3s, the fat that's best for your child's brain. Nature designed it so. These fats are different for every mammal. Cow's milk is meant for baby cows; mouse milk is meant for baby mice.

It has in fact been proven that breast feeding your child for two years or longer leads to the biggest and best brain for your child.

Although the American Academy of Pediatrics and the World health organization both recommend at least six months of breast feeding, they advocate doing even more than that. But only about 50% of mothers participate even to that degree.

Astonishingly, just last week, the US tried to persuade the WHO to water down or scrap a simple resolution meant to encourage breast feeding in underdeveloped countries.

The effort was anti-science, pro-fast food industry. It was borne of love for industry money, against the interests of public health.

The baby formula industry makes about $70 million a year. Sadly, as knowledge of the benefits of breast feeding has been spreading throughout the world, industry has been fighting back. Our government and industry frankly do not care.

As expected, President Trump said on Twitter that women need access to baby formula because of malnutrition. But fast food and sugar addiction are actually the main problem, even in poor countries. Most children in poor countries eat a lot better than we do. Just look at the children and you'll see.

Almost all women produce breast milk that is much healthier than formula for the baby. After reading *Whitewash* by Joe Keon, I doubt you will be feeding your child cow's milk ever again. The book is full of scientific references.

Breast milk has less allergens and toxins, resulting in lower rates of otitis, allergic reactions, and lung infections.

Unethical marketing practices on the part of the milk industry are well documented, and the information promulgated by the federal government is not scientific. False advertising in the US and unscientific recommendations by the government have led to a decrease in breast feeding, especially in underdeveloped countries.

The lives of our children are at stake.

Some formula has nutrients added, but it is still inferior to mother's milk, which is well-researched and scientifically proven.

Ecuador was going to endorse the use of mother's milk to the World Health Organization, but the US threatened them with withdrawal of crucial military aid unless they dropped their recommendation.

Common sense will ultimately triumph in this round of plain old bullying by the US. But the US is also trying the same tactics in other countries.

Enough Is Enough:
The Fruit Juice Delusion

Federal guidelines state that half of our daily fruit servings may be consumed as 100% fruit juice. The same misguided advice affects the school breakfast eaten by 14 million American children daily, and the school lunch program that feeds 30 million daily.

There is no regulation of sugar in school meals, which is unbelievable considering the increasing obesity rates in our school children. Obesity is causing a massive increase in many chronic diseases at a young age, especially diabetes, not just type one but mainly type 2.

A single breakfast of juice, milk, and sweet cereal or pastry can easily exceed a child's entire daily sugar quota .

At lunch, manufacturer's offer brightly hued frozen juice cups that can stand in not just for half of children's weekly fruit intake but also for red and orange vegetables, squandering an opportunity for children to experience these foods in their whole state.

Children don't need juice. They need to eat the apple, orange, tomato, or banana without industrial sprays. They need the fiber. Fruit juice is full of sugar. And sugar is the booger and the hooker.

Damaging Our Children's Brains with Sports and Child Abuse

As a neurosurgeon, I saw so many children over the years who had significant injuries to their bodies, including permanent ones to their brains.

I mean children who never spoke again, were paralyzed, had to have a breathing tube in place, and if they didn't die, lived in a nursing home the rest of their lives—all because of trauma inflicted by a parent, relative, boyfriend, girlfriend, or criminal. Sometimes, the abuse is mainly psychological, as in the case of a parent who's an alcoholic or drug addict. Some have to breathe in the toxic air of cigarettes or marijuana.

This is not something I witnessed only on occasion. I saw it on a daily basis. Child abuse is tragically common and if witnessed needs to be reported immediately—it's the law. Being merely a witness, even if you don't participate, makes you equally guilty. Most of the time, someone in the family knew of behavior like this and did not stand up for the child.

A concussion results from shaking the brain in a way that changes the normal action of the neurons. Scans of the concussed brain are usually normal. Most sufferers complain of temporary memory loss, temporary loss of consciousness, and short-term cognitive impairment, fully recovering within 24 to 48 hours.

Every year, about 4 million concussions are reported from all types of sports activities through the National Center for Disease Control and Prevention. But many injuries are not reported and so are not represented in these statistics.

Concussions are the leading cause of brain injury in the 15-24 age group. In 1997, at least 50 children died from sports-related head injuries on the field.

It is estimated that 20% of teenage athletes receive a concussion every year.

Concussions occur in all types of sports and recreational activities, even some that don't involve a lot of heavy contact.

I remember as a neurosurgeon I once treated an 18-year-old girl who presented with extreme drowsiness. She was nearly unconscious at about four in the morning. I asked a family member whether she had suffered a head injury in the last few days and they said no. There was extensive blood on the surface of the temporal and occipital lobes of the brain. I wondered if she had a brain aneurysm. But the angiogram was negative. I spoke to the family some more and found out the day before she had been doing a lot of twists and turns on a single ski on Lake Wawasee.

This indicated to me that the girl's 3-pound brain, made largely from fat, had been rotating at a different speed than the hard skull and that surrounded it. Her brain's surface blood vessels had thus fallen victim to Newton's third law of thermodynamics. A significant number of brain cells and brain fibers had been bruised and torn. She eventually recovered but don't you wonder what her long-term outlook might look like? Will she have dementia at a younger age? We certainly know the story foam football players.

Concussions occur when an athlete skull is met with great force, or rotational forces are applied to it. It can be a bat, baseball, soccer ball, volleyball, even a golf ball. I've seen a number of serious golf ball injuries, including one that resulted in a patient's death.

Concussions are caused by two different forces: the first are linear and the second rotational. The latter are more forceful.

Concussions are accompanied by five main symptoms: headache, nausea, vomiting, visual problems, and dizziness. But symptoms can also include emotional issues like sadness or depression. Sleep disturbances are common. Also, memory loss and cognitive impairment may occur but are generally temporary. Then again, anyone who's had a number of concussions can have long-term memory loss or even seizures. It's the number that counts.

Children's brains are not fully developed until age 25, so any type of injury—physical, mental, or chemical—can have an accentuated effect and last for a lifetime.

I read a scientific article recently about how repeated hits from soccer balls lead to cognitive decline in later years, if not immediately. This has now been scientifically proven. So, allowing your child to play soccer may actually be allowing child abuse. I recently listened to a lecture by a doctor who is famous for promoting the idea of Cognitive Traumatic Impairment (CTI) from football injuries, and he talked about soccer injuries being nearly as common and severe.

Sometimes, cognitive tests are used on the field, like having the player repeat six digits and then repeat them backwards. It's a simple test but certainly very limited.

You can see boxing would be even riskier than sports like football and soccer. Boxing is the only sport where direct blows to the head are repeated and often render the athlete unconscious. All of us have witnessed the decline of some famous boxers.

Some places now don't allow a child under age 14 to play soccer, because the younger brain is more likely to suffer permanent injuries.
But you can have a concussion from volleyball, usually it is related to spiking the ball, and these injuries are significant. Baseball bats, baseballs, and softballs can of course result in significant permanent injuries and even deaths.

What's a parent to do? They have to sign the permission slip, but they can end up with a permanently injured child, or a dead one. Then again, there are children who are highly motivated to excel at sports, which might keep them away from other bad habits like alcohol, cigarettes, marijuana, etc. They're more likely to be healthy with good exercise habits which may last a lifetime.

My mother let me play football for six weeks; that clearly it was a mistake. I weighed only 130 pounds, and the physical punishment was more than I could stand. I went to a very small school, and social pressure made me do it. I was a good baseball and tennis player, but you can see the problem. Fortunately, I was kicked off the team. It made me very happy that I had a good excuse to survive the social aspect.

Knowing what I know now, I would not let my child play football or soccer. Tennis, golf, pickle ball, walking and running, dancing, singing and acting are good enough for me.

Wrestling can also be traumatic. Then again, every wrestling child I've ever met was very disciplined. I don't recall seeing major head injuries or paralysis in wrestlers, although they certainly could occur.

Neonatal Abstinence Syndrome (NAS)

Neonatal Abstinence Syndrome (NAS) is a condition experienced by newborns resulting from exposure to opioids in utero. Infants born to mothers who use opioids while pregnant are at increased risk for negative neonatal, and possibly lifetime, outcomes.

Symptoms apparent at birth include increased irritability, spasticity, tremors, difficulty eating, vomiting, watery stools, seizures, and respiratory distress. Many sufferers are underweight. Of infants exposed to opioids in the womb, 60-80% will have symptoms.

There has been a steady rise in the number off NAS cases nationally since the year 2000, paralleling the rise in prescription opioids and heroin use. I would think it would also parallel the use of marijuana. According to my conversation with a local judge, almost every case that she's prosecuting for opioids involved a user who began with marijuana.

NAS is also underdiagnosed. The usual hospital stay for a normal infant is about two days; the hospital stay for an infant with NAS is about 16 days. Also, the mother may need treatment because she may be addicted to opioids.

Breast feeding must also be delayed in these cases. Mother's milk is the best food for the development of a child's brain, so being deprived of it at birth could have lifetime effects. Mother's milk is the healthiest thing you can feed any child. The healthiest child's brain is fed by mother's milk. It has more of the good fats called omega-3s.

The hospital cost of a NAS infant was about $66,000 in 2013.

Also, the mother will in most cases be faced with legal and criminal problems and cost. That certainly will effect the newborn infant. They may even be taken out of the home.

In my 50 years of practicing neurosurgery, I saw many children affected by NAS. I also saw far too much child abuse, including many cases where the parents had their child removed from the home. You can imagine the effect of that on the child, as well as the mother and father. Many of these children have to enter the welfare system and go into foster care.

Many of the children who have NAS suffer from impaired brain development, with cognitive issues, seizures, lowered IQ, and even paralysis. Almost every one of them is very anxious. These and other mental issues are common consequences.

The opioids affect a child's DNA and rewrite their genetic scripts. If the mother is consuming alcohol, smoking, using opioids or marijuana, they all affect the genetic script of the infant. Essentially, the father, and especially the mother, are harming and possibly killing their offspring with their unhealthy habits.

The field of epigenetics has shown scientifically that the lifestyle of the mother and father have tremendous effects on the infant and its future.

When you are writing your child's genetic script with your own addictions, you're causing great harm to your offspring. You have to wonder what the future holds for these children.

There is great value in prevention. For the vast majority of women, drug use or abuse begins long before they become pregnant. Therefore, key drivers for achieving healthier pregnancies and births, and better child safety outcomes, is in helping women of childbearing age to have better access to effective birth control methods. Engaging women of childbearing age who have substance abuse disorders to seek treatment before they become pregnant is very important as well. Broad community approaches to preventing opioid abuse disorders are underway in many states and should be expanded to target opioid use during pregnancy. Many agencies are focusing on the unique needs of pregnant women with opioid abuse disorders. Then again, these young mothers may also have problems with alcohol or marijuana or other addictions, and we must keep that in mind.

What is FASD?

When development of a fetus's central nervous system is disturbed or interrupted, lifetime neurological abnormalities can develop, including movement, impaired cognitive functions, seizures, etc. Alcohol consumption, even before conception, but especially during pregnancy, has the ability to disrupt the normal development of the fetal brain. Alcohol is a toxin and a poison.

The impact of alcohol exposure leads to a spectrum of harm under the umbrella term Fetal Alcohol Spectrum Disorders.

1. Fetal Alcohol Syndrome (FAS)
2. Partial Fetal Alcohol Syndrome (PFAS)
3. Alcohol-Related Neurodevelopmental Disorder (ARND)
4. Alcohol-Related Birth Defects (ARBD)
5. Neurodevelopmental Disorder as a Result of Prenatal Exposure to Alcohol (ND-PEA)

Symptoms of FASD include: inconsistent memory and recall, slow and inconsistent cognitive and auditory processing, mental illnesses, poor emotional regulation, low self-esteem, difficulties in controlling impulsive behaviors, difficulties in understanding rules and regulations, poor motor coordination, sleep and eating disorders, and an inability to read social cues or predict outcomes.

This disability is largely unrecognized within communities, schools, childcare services, adoption agencies, and many times it goes unseen and undiagnosed.

Many of these children have mental health disorders, 90% end up with alcoholic addiction, 60%, have trouble with the law which leads to an incarceration rate of 60%. They may engage in inappropriate sexual behaviors, 50% have difficulty with employment stability, and 80% are unable to live independently.

The effects of alcohol on the brain, even with these disorders, are reversible a majority of the time. My years as a neurosurgeon visually demonstrated the tremendous amount of brain volume lost to alcohol in my patients. The physiological nature of alcohol during pregnancy is not affected by race, religion, or culture. No matter who you are, alcohol consumption before and especially during pregnancy has serious effects on the infant, involving every aspect of development, not just the brain.

"Fetal Alcohol Syndrome" was first described in the *Lancet* medical journal 40 years ago. They are even comments about the condition in the Bible. Aristotle in 400 BC suggested that children of alcoholics were often morose. The Royal College of Physicians in London described children borne of alcoholic mothers as weak, feeble, and anxious.

Science has revealed that alcohol affects our neurotransmitters. These neurotransmitters function in a brain to carry messages or signals throughout the body and control fundamental human behaviors such as thought processes, behaviors, and emotions. The brain has around 100 billion neurons and nerve cells and around 100 trillion synaptic connections. It is synaptic connections that are vital to living a healthy and normal life.

Alcohol has the ability to increase dopamine, a neurotransmitter that creates the feeling of pleasure. Therefore, its affects are visible in the brain of an adult, but it has even more effects on the newly developing brain of a child. The metabolism rate in a child is completely different and susceptible to a lot more harm. Adults may have a hangover and recover by noon the next day, but it also causes cellular damage with cell loss, but still not as much as a fetus.

Due to alcohol's rapid solubility in water, it can cross cell membranes, which are made from water, very quickly. The placenta acts as a selective barrier. Alcohol is easily passed by diffusion from the maternal blood into the fetal bloodstream by this mechanism. A key factor, remember, is that humans vary widely in their ability to absorb and eliminate alcohol. This can be a factor in alcohol use in pregnancy. Absorption and elimination rates of alcohol may be quicker in some people's genetic makeup and may be a protective factor to the unborn child in others.

Of all the substances of abuse that women may use during pregnancy, I'll call this the most serious, with the most long-lasting effects.

Fetal Alcohol Syndrome (FAS)

Fetal Alcohol Spectrum Disorders is an umbrella term which is used to describe a range of mental, physical, and neural behavioral birth defects that result from alcohol exposure during pregnancy. It is one of the leading causes of preventable birth defects and developmental disabilities in the world today. FASD is a permanent brain injury to the developing fetus due to alcohol being a teratogen, which is a substance that disrupts the developing fetus. Alcohol enters the bloodstream of the fetus from the mother's bloodstream without any filter or barrier, and the toxic elements of alcohol harm the fetus. Alcohol is more dangerous than many of the illicit drugs that are used throughout society today.

FASD in itself is not a clinical diagnostic term but an umbrella term to encompass a constellation of effects that can occur when alcohol is consumed in pregnancy. These effects vary widely in how they present in children who have been exposed to alcohol in the womb. The syndrome is prevalent in our families, schools, foster care, and adoption services.

Fetal alcohol exposure has been present for thousands of years but it is only recently that a true understanding of the mechanism of harm has emerged due to the rapid advances of medical research. FASD can involve a range of malformations, including facial features, but by far the most significant is permanent organic brain injury. It is now clear that a child exposed to alcohol may have a range of intellectual and behavioral outcomes that remain with them across the complete lifespan.

One of the conditions under the umbrella term of FASD is Fetal Alcohol Syndrome (FAS). This condition is marked by the appearance of craniofacial abnormalities, small head circumference, and a number of other deficiencies and difficulties. It is more understood due to the visible nature of the disability. Less well known, however, are the other conditions under the umbrella which leave many children undiagnosed or misdiagnosed due to lack of awareness. This can have a range of effects along a spectrum, which has a huge impact on the individual and family who may struggle to gain access to services and supports which could help them deal with the consequences of alcohol exposure.

Thousands of studies conducted in many different nations have found that children born after alcohol exposure during pregnancy can have lifelong disabilities Yet for reasons unknown, this public health information is still ignored, disregarded, and even rejected by academics, physicians, and politicians. For example, 80% of the pregnant mothers in Scotland still consume alcohol regularly. The result of this lack of recognition is that an estimated 1 million children born annually around the world suffer from a neurobehavioral condition that will impact them in the home, school, and throughout their lifespans.

Currently, there is no universal screening for FASD in maternity hospitals. The US and Canada have been leading the way in providing an understanding of this disability. The most reliable statistics emerge from various US studies converge on a figure of 9 births per 1000 that are affected by Prenatal Alcohol Exposure (PAE). The incidence rate of FASD may be higher in some regions, with some studies suggesting that the rate in high-risk populations like foster care and adoption cases may be as high as 10-15 per 1000.

Significant medical advances have occurred over many years to address the negative health consequences of modern hedonistic lifestyles with drug and alcohol use across all sectors of society. But these treatments can't undo the work. The effects of smoking, cigarettes, marijuana, opioid, and alcohol use present great challenges to our healthcare system. I encourage you to read *Understanding Fetal Alcohol Spectrum Disorder* by Maria Catterick and Liam Curam.

I am trying to spread awareness by writing this book, but these authors and other professionals in allied health positions, as well as parents and the people who take care of children, also have an obligation to spread the word about alcohol and what it does to the fetal brain. My own experience of 45 years in neurosurgery and taking out many blood clots from the brains of alcoholics tells me, "Alcohol is a killer of brain cells." It literally destroys the brain, with effects so severe that most never fully recover; they're missing huge parts of their brain.

From the personal accounts of birth by mothers, adoptive parents, and foster parents, I have learned that it is without question that FASD needs a multi-model approach within local communities to ensure fulfilling futures for children and adults living with this lifelong condition. As a disability, FASD is pervasive within the systems of social services, education, health, and justice. There is an urgent need to work collectively and strategically at all levels of society to create prevention policies and provide services for those affected.

Infancy

They can be a variety of signs and symptoms associated with FASD. An infant actually may have signs of withdrawal. Some will have unusual facial features including eyes, lips, and skull shape. There may be an unusual pattern of alertness, and irregular wake-sleep cycles. Failure to thrive and increased susceptibility to infections are common issues, along with feeding problems, such as difficulty sucking and acid reflux, difficulty with textures, gorging on food, indifference to food. Head banging or walking with gross motor delays can also occur. A high-pitched cry, however, is the classic symptom. The infant may not have typical eye contact or dislike physical contact. This list of indicators is not exclusive to FASD, but they are good cause for further investigation. If the infant is experiencing withdrawal, it may need medication and support by cuddling and gentle handling in a quieter and less stimulating environment.

Many of these infants need a big support system. This can include a geneticist to help make an accurate diagnosis. A neuropsychologist can help by doing cognitive assessments, such as the Weschler Intelligence Scale for children, which establishes baselines of functioning. Another common assessment tool is the Vineland Adaptive Behavior Scale (VABS). Likewise, a physiotherapist and a good family doctor or pediatrician will be needed.

Prevention is of course the best treatment. Frankly, we need to teach the children how to be healthy in the home, but unfortunately that may not happen in many settings, especially when the parents are consumers of alcohol, marijuana, opioids, and alcohol.

To reach the most people, I personally think education should start at an early age in the school setting. About 20 years ago, we were able to cut the opioid epidemic by about 50% thanks to a very active Dr. William Bennett. He also wrote a great book on preventing addiction of all types in children I highly recommend it. Also, I would highly recommend reading a book called *Understanding Fetal Alcohol Spectrum Disorder* by Maria Catterick and Liam Curran. I quote from them liberally.

For best results: "Prevention is the cure."

Sudden Infant Death Syndrome (SIDS)

Sudden Infant Death Syndrome is the most common cause of death in the first 12 months of the life of an infant.

It is more common in males and there is an increased incidence in the first 6 months of life and during cold weather. African Americans are more commonly affected. Native Americans also have an increased rate.

There is increased incidence with babies who sleep on their stomachs.

Families that smoke or use drugs and alcohol also have an increased risk of finding their infant dead in their crib, obviously a horrifying situation. What clearly makes it even worse is when the parents find out they contributed to the death of their child.

It has been recommended that infants sleep on their backs the first 12 months of their life at least. Not all SIDS cases can be prevented, but a high percentage can. So prevention is the cure in most cases. Avoiding second-hand smoke is critical. Of course, avoiding opioids, alcohol, and marijuana is very important for the mother and father because they are rewriting the genetic code of the infant even before conception and during intrauterine development, as well as throughout the life in the crib and growing into childhood.

Once again, prevention is the cure.

The Undeclared War against Children

Violence against children has been manifested in every conceivable manner, from physical or emotional abuse to neglect, overwork, and sexual exploitation. In 1895, the Society for the Prevention of Cruelty to Children listed the implements of abuse against London children: boots, fans, shovels, straps, ropes, thongs, pokers, fire, and boiling water. Children were held in the clutches of idle drunkards, vagrants. Little girls were victims of sexual abuse. Children were little slaves put to grueling labor and displayed in circuses, where they were treated as monstrosities at traveling shows.

As a neurosurgeon, I remember seeing a five-year-old patient whose mother kept on insisting there was something wrong with the shot her child was receiving for hydrocephalus, even though I could see it was functioning quite fine and the child had no symptoms. Then I took a detailed history and found out the mother had been pushing further surgeries on the child with another neurosurgeon in another city. This is called Munchausen syndrome by proxy. This mother put her child through a living hell. She was getting pleasure out of her activity. I have also seen intentional poisoning of children by their mothers and fathers, and it is a form of child abuse.

In ancient times, when might made right, the infant had no rights until the right to life was ritually bestowed. Until then, the infant was a non-entity, disposed of with as little compunction as an aborted fetus. The newborn had to be acknowledged by the father, but what the father produced was his to do with as he wished. Children's rights were always a prerogative of parenthood. As head of the family, the father had the ultimate authority; even the mother was subordinate to his wishes. We are speaking about hundreds of years ago.

The child was a non-person in some societies until it received a name. Some North American Indians threw newborns into a pool of water and saved it only if it rose to the surface and cried. The Christian child did not get heavenly recognition until he was baptized a Christian; at that time the name was assigned. The soul of a child that died before baptism was believed not to go to heaven but would rather be condemned to everlasting limbo. The body of such a child could not be buried in hallowed ground but instead was disposed of in the same manner as a dead dog or cat. This is all well explained in a book called *The Battered Child* by Ray E. Helfer and Ruth S. Kempe. The original guidebook on the subject was written by Kempe's deceased husband, who made this subject of child abuse his life-long passion.

A few hundred years ago, illegitimate children were all beyond the law and thus especially vulnerable to abuse. If they weren't firstborns, they had to do without the benefit of a career in the clergy or an inheritance. Meanwhile, in the Middle Ages, only the children of priests and bishops were permitted to marry, but the parents had to buy a proper dispensation to make their children legitimate.

In the 16, 17, and 1800s, children were especially exploited for their labor. Child labor took root under the apprenticeship system through work houses and orphanages, as well as in industry. In these places, cruel punishment was inflicted on the children until an outcry on the part of the community led to the idea of public health being born. Johan Pedo Frank (1745-1821), the German physician who founded the science of public health, was shocked by the agrarian child labor used in continental viticulture, which resulted in youngsters becoming deformed and miss happen. Frank advocated laws in the 18th Century to provide age limits for specific kinds of work and prohibiting the forcing of weak children to do the heavy work of artisans. Only older boys would be allowed to do the labor of grown men.

But such laws had to wait another century before they were enacted. The guilds of the Middle Ages regulated the work of children, not out of compassion, but to prevent competitive cheap labor. A government statue in 1562 regulated control over provinces, confining children to indentured servitude for seven years, a system of enslavement that lasted until 1815. In the 17 Century, six-year-old children toiled in the clothing industry, and a great demand burst forth for children in factories after the Industrial Revolution. Early in the 18th Century, this led to further excruciating exploitation. "Pity the poor creatures," wrote someone in 1801, when child labor was viewed as beneficial not only to society but to the child as well. They were battered both physically and psychologically. As punishment, these children were forced to bend their heads down between their knees so that blood front flowed from the nose and ears.

There was no protection in the mills for children when they were mercilessly beaten or overworked. This was the case until the child labor laws instigated reforms doing the 19th Century. Children were transported to the American colonies in droves to bring apprenticed until the age of 24. Pauper children were sold by the alms houses into apprenticeships and treated atrociously. Colonial newspapers constantly advertised runaway children. As late as 1866, Mississippi's legislative report was hailing child labor as a boon to society. Writing on child labor laws in 1891, Abraham Jacoby, the father of American pediatrics, cried out against the employment of near babies in the mines and as chimney sweeps. Inexpensive child labor was supplied to greedy industry by the poorhouses. The working child was even more abused in rural areas.

Alcohol not only harms the unborn child but also the child nurtured by an alcoholic mother. When the British National Society for the Prevention of Cruelty to Children sorted out the victims of neglect, about 90% were neglected because of excessive drinking by one or both parents. Alcoholic mothers lost all sense of parenthood, their homes were seldom clean, their children rarely washed. Unsurprisingly, these children quickly swelled infant mortality rate.

Child marriage, especially for girls, was widely prevalent in the past, and some cultures still do it. Some Hindus consider it disgraceful for girls to remain unmarried until menstruation, and premenstrual copulation was extensively practiced under coverage of marriage. About 20% of these marriages involved girls of 12 or 13. Deaths of these children during their first sexual acts were not rare, but they were usually concealed.

The London Society for the Protection of Young Females recorded children no older than 11 were trapped in houses of prostitution. These girls were not permitted to leave until they were old and "broken in." Some children became pregnant at age 9 and 10.

Rape was common in the unbridled days of the past, especially during wartime. It occurs in the Bible, as well as in Roman history, and it played a prominent part in the drama of historic violence.

Children's rights advanced slowly overtime. Protective services for children were slow to develop. Even the Bible commands, "Do not sin against the child."

Children have also historically been put in private foster homes. Here, the kids were often subjected to maltreatment and neglect, with no more than a sporting chance of survival. Eighty percent of illegitimate children under the care of a nurse in London during the 19th Century perished. As a matter of fact, some nurses had a reputation as skilled baby killers. The Germans called them "Angel makers." A grim report of 1881 stated that 31% of illegitimate children died under foster care. A favorite method of doing away with an infant was to give him or her nothing but a pacifier soaked in brandy. In spite of such gross irregularities, foundlings fared better under foster care than in foundling institutions.

Child Abuse as a Pediatric Problem

Except for medical cases of injured children, the problem of the battered child in the past ordinarily was not the concern of the physician. The mission was to heal the sick, not to deal with social problems. Fortunately, that has changed tremendously.

I practiced full-time neurosurgery for 45 years and treated many abused children for neurological injuries. Many were frankly devastating. The laws are so strict today that I witnessed even the slightest suspicion of abuse leading to the removal of a mother's most precious gifts, her children, many a time, on the spot. They just disappeared based on state and federal law. I feel sorry for many of them and fully understand the potential danger to the children. My wife was even on the board call SCAN, a wonderful organization that tries to help children. She resigned after a time because she could not take the stories of abuse and still sleep at night. God bless our neighbor Ruth, who has made it her life's mission to work with this great organization. Please contribute some money to SCAN (as I do regularly).

Originally, pediatricians treated only those with medical problems, but eventually they started getting involved with the social aspects also. In 1882, the New York State Medical Society formed a committee to cooperate with the Society for the Prevention of Cruelty to Children in formulating legislation to improve child labor laws.

Things moved far more quickly when x-rays became available. Now, you could see the fractured bones in the children. Radiology appeared just at the dawn of the 20th Century. Pediatricians paid attention to the babies until hospital x-ray departments in New York started gazing at the medical evidence and doing something about it. The radiologist wasn't an adept pediatrician, but he was able to relate these unexplained x-ray findings to clinical nurses. They soon recognized that multiple fractures were due to trauma, but they were unable to convince his colleagues the parents might be the instrument of this trauma.

In 1946, Dr. Caffey publish a paper called "Mortal Fractures in the Long Bones of Infants Suffering from Chronic Subdural Hematoma." This attracted the attention of pediatricians to the ramifications of child abuse. Unfortunately, this issue remained known to no more than a small group for several years. In 1955, it was at last generally conceded that multiple injuries to children were committed willfully, and the profession began to pay attention. Dr. Kempe studied all the different features of child abuse from 1951-1958, and linked child abuse to pediatrics. I take my hat off to him because he was a member of the program committee of the American Academy of Pediatrics, and when he became chairman in 1961, he organized a multidisciplinary conference with the title of *The Battered Child Syndrome*. This set ablaze an impassioned outburst on behalf of abused children. A bandwagon effect was generated. The Children's Bureau came to fill the void with generous grants for the study of the subject, and the American Humane Society carried out surveys, issued pertinent publications, and hosted several conventions and symposia. A "Child Abuse" heading first appeared in the quarterly cumulative index *Medicus* in 1965, under which about 40 published articles were listed.

In Great Britain, a 1966 study by the National Society for the Prevention of Cruelty to Children found that more than half of abused children were less than the year-old and battered by their own mothers. The rest were battered by their fathers, stepfathers, and boyfriends' of the mothers. Almost all required hospitalization, over half of them on a repeating basis. The society set up centers with programs for corrective mothering, patterned after those set in motion by the Denver group and named The London Center Kempe House to honor the pioneering efforts of Doctor Kempe's group.

Child protection has shifted from the pending list to the therapeutic. Slowly, but steadily, emphasis has turned to rescuing children and prosecuting offending parents and getting them rehab and treatment, helping families in crisis, preserving good standards of parental behavior, and providing basic needs for optimum care of children and harmonious family relationships.

Now, as new tech is taking over, there is more recognition of children at risk and better efforts at rehabilitation for trouble families. These programs aim to preserve the natural development of the child with the acknowledgement of child abuse as a pediatric responsibility to address. New life has been instilled in the campaign for children's rights.

I personally wonder if we're not overdoing it a bit. In my time as a neurosurgeon, I saw so many children leaving their mothers' love forever. Then again, a lot of people know a lot more about it than I do. I would just like for them to keep that in mind.

Screen Time Linked to ADHD

Researchers are starting to link scrolling, swiping, surfing, and streaming with other habits that consume the adolescent mind, along with the minds of some adults. An average American parent might well watch and wonder if they are living with a robot.

I see teenagers walking in front of me when driving almost every day. I'm trying to avoid hitting them, possibly injuring or killing them.

The research is coming in proving that teens who spend more time on their ever-growing number of digital media platforms exhibit a mounting array of attention difficulties and impulse-control problems.

A study of 2,500 high school students in Los Angeles found a rising number of symptoms linked to Attention Deficit Disorder (ADHD). It was about a 10% connection

Another study, published by the American Medical Association, revealed that 95% of adolescents have access to a smart phone and 45% said they are online "almost constantly." It should make us all worry.

Generally, ADHD was thought to start in early childhood and last across a lifetime. With symptoms including impulsivity, hyperactivity, and difficulty sustaining attention, ADHD is estimated to effect about 7% of children and adolescents.

Now, doctors are diagnosing it more in older teens and even adults, and in actuality the risk does last over a lifetime. This raises the possibility that for some ADHD symptoms are brought on or exacerbated by the hyper-stimulating action of winking, painting, vibrating, or following graphic on any of the digital offerings that is close and available on the wireless device in their hand.

The printed literature is full of research findings showing that excessive use of digital media has consequences for our developing brain. Our brains are generally thought to not be fully developed until age 25. And look at all that we do to our children's brains as they are growing.

It has also been found that children who spend a lot of time on digital media are less happy. They have found more depression and even some suicides.

Researchers are starting to use a “cumulative media-use index” for kids between ages one and 14. Four out of five students acknowledge high-frequency use of at least one activity, including 54% who told researchers they checked social media many times per day. Two-thirds engage in high-frequency use of up to four online activities at some point during the study’s course.
Up to 4.82 or 6.9% of the subjects met this criterion.

If these kids acknowledge having any six criteria, they were considered to be “ADHD symptom-positive.” About 5 to 6.9% of the subjects met these criteria.

It is quite clear that a parent needs to have a strong relationship with their children and regulate their activity on cell phones and iPads. The hours spent watching TV should also be on the list. I remember seeing a family in my office years ago where are all the children, along with the mother and father, where on a digital device and never looked up while I was discussing the dad’s pending surgery. On a postoperative visit to this family, I witnessed the same scenario, and that was over 10 years ago. Can you imagine the situation for this family now?

What My Eyes See

I just finished reading an excellent book, *What the Eyes Don't See*, by Dr. Mona Hannah Attisha. It's about the lead found in the drinking water of Flint Michigan.

Lead is a known toxin to the brain, especially the brain of a newborn child in the first 18 months of life. The heightened risk continues as children's brains develop till about age 25.

To save money, the state and health departments ordered a switch from water that originated from Lake Heron to the Flint River. The local, regional, state, and federal agencies, as well as the majority of political figures, didn't do their jobs, resulting in elevated lead levels in the population's supply of drinking water. That started a huge resistance movement that Dr. Attisha fought on a daily basis. Eventually, she came out the winner.

Who knows for certain what the effects will be on the developing brains of these children, as well as the adults. Clearly, many children were harmed. Public health officials did not step up to bat and solve the problem early on. They instead showed a serious disregard for the people involved. You may even wonder if there were some racial motives.

It was an environmental and public health disaster, one of the biggest of this century. It is the story of a government poisoning its own citizens and then lying about it. The very people who are responsible for keeping us, and especially our children, safe cared more about money.

The crisis of lead in the water effected the brains of our precious and vulnerable children, who drank the water and ate meals cooked with it, and babies who drank formula mixed with that water. The government tried hard to convince parents the water was safe, even though they knew it wasn't. We witnessed a breakdown in democracy, accentuated by efforts to save money, exacerbated by inequality and environmental injustice. The poison water disproportionately affected the poor and the black communities. It resulted from an abandonment of civic responsibility and our deep obligation as human beings to care and provide for one another.

I personally believe it is the same kind of logic we are applying to the type of food we feed our children, which results in poor health and many chronic diseases that could easily be avoided. Public health education is generally very poor and affects certain ethnic and racial groups a great deal more than others. The funding of schools is much different in cities than the suburbs, in spite of a lot of state and federal money being involved. Let's face it, most districts have segregated schools process in a way that affects school quality and public health education.

The Flint, Michigan story is one of resilience, where leaders like Dr. Attisha stepped up to bat and managed to change the city for the betterment of all. Despite the many harms to our children I've brought to light in this book, I'm doing my best to point out changes that all of us can help bring about to improve their future.

Dr. Attisha from Flint, Michigan and I have a sense of mission.

Just like Dr. Attisha, I feel a sense of mission as a physician to educate people on how to improve their lives and avoid most illnesses through lifestyle choices and habits, which I do almost daily. Using radio, TV, lectures, lifestyle coaching, demonstrating my own good health habits, writing books, and talking about what I actually see and have tried to change. As expected, that may not be always appreciated.

When Dr. Attisha would hear a crying baby, it would give her a sense of mission. She had inside herself a primal drive to help others thrive. She suggests in her book that maybe all pediatricians have this drive to some extent. She states she isn't a fanatic when it comes to protecting all kids, but when she sees children in danger through no fault of their own, she gets a little mad.

You can see where she's coming from when you read about how she discovered the drinking water of Flint, Michigan had the lead in it. That's how I feel as I'm trying to spread the message that it is a lot easier to prevent Type II Diabetes, along with the 50 diseases attached to it, than to treat them after they've developed. Attisha quotes Frederick Douglass: "It's easier to build strong children than to repair a broken man." I agree with that 1000%.

Can you imagine that when the lease was up on her old clinic, they moved the pediatric center into a one-of-a-kind building with soaring ceilings and a spectacular sunlight, above a year-round farmers market and just a few steps from the central bus stop? Because she dealt mainly with the disadvantaged population, many of whom did not have cars?

She says that a kid born in Flint will live 15 years less than a kid born in a neighboring suburban house. This again demonstrates why I feel we are harming and unfortunately even killing our children. At least I know after reading Dr. Attisha's great book that somebody cares.

Social Determinants of Health

We can call them adverse childhood experiences or toxic stressors. A child's first years of life are the most critical in their development. The multiple stressors of home, social situation, poverty, racism, and environment chronically activate stress hormones which affect neural connections in the brain through neural plasticity, especially up to age 25 or so.

A large study of 17,000 HMO members found that the more adverse childhood experiences or toxic stressors a child is subjected to the greater the chances of long-term physical and behavioral health issues.

As a matter of fact, if a child has 6 or more of these stressors it drops life expectancy by 20 years. Pediatricians aren't just looking at a child's physical condition on the day of an exam room visit; they are also looking at the future. Dr. Attisha points out that her pediatric residents need to read the most up-to-date literature and science from the field of toxic stress, neurodevelopment, and resilience.

Can you imagine the first thing Dr. Attisha does with the new pediatric residents is to take them on a tour of Flint, Michigan? She wants them to know where the patients are coming from. All I can do is clap my hands and tap dance to one of my favorite songs. She is playing my music. In fact, when I teach some college students, I use poetry, singing, and tap dancing. She also has her residents view *Unnatural Causes*, a seven-hour PBS documentary about socioeconomic and racial disparities in healthcare in America and their root causes.

Harming and Killing Our Children with Guns

This is not a chapter about your right to own a gun. I think that issue was settled a few years ago. It's about how we are currently harming and killing our children, because this nation has about 400 million guns, and we are being careless with them: not properly storing them, not teaching proper use of them, using them in criminal activity, not restricting access to weapons that can put out a lot of bullets very rapidly, not controlling the ownership of guns by the mentally impaired or people with a criminal history. I could go on and on, but you get the idea.

The interesting thing is that there are many nations with very low gun ownership, and as a result the number of gun deaths and injuries per capita is a much less than in America. After a single mass shooting, Australia for example bought back a lot of the guns in the country, and their already low incidence of accidental shootings and suicides decreased even further.

About 33% of the people in our country own the 400 million or so guns that we have. School mass shootings, usually perpetrated by mentally impaired young males, have continued. I suspect before long we'll have another one.

Over half the gun injuries and deaths are due to suicide attempts, which are about 90% successful. We have about 45000 gun deaths per year, and over 50% are suicides, mainly by males. Suicide by girls is only about 10% successful, because they tend to use less lethal means like drug overdoses.

So, the availability of guns does make a great deal of difference, especially in the home. If there is a gun in the home, it is four times as likely that a family member would be injured or killed by it than an intruder—something most gun owners are not aware of. Proper gun storage and education about usage among all family members is absolutely critical.

Workplace suicidal shootings are 91% successful. School shooters are usually males, so a availability of guns for mentally impaired individuals comes into play.

Domestic violence also increases the rate of gun injuries and deaths.

Mass shootings are those in which at least four individuals are injured or killed by an assailant. Most criminal violence involving guns takes place in a single event, with one or two victims, like criminal activity in general.

The US suicide death rate with firearms is 2,415 cases per 100,000 people per year, which means we rank as number four for all reporting nations. The US has high rates of firearm homicide and suicide in comparison to other western nations. The male rate is six times higher than the female rate.

It is interesting that deaths represent 3.2% of all victims, while 96.8% of shooting result in injuries. As a neurosurgeon for 45 years, I took care of a lot of them. Many where paralyzed or demented for life, resulting in horrible lives and tremendous cost, both to the families and to the government.

Bullying definitely plays a part in gun violence, especially among children. Many schools are reacting and changing the social structure of the environment as best as possible. Many children are now emotionally impaired or depressed because of conflicts between the mother and father. Let's face it, the nation is running a 50% divorce rate at least. You can imagine the effect on the children.

In the year 2010, 340,000 violent crimes were committed with guns as the weapon.

Approximately 675 people were unintentionally killed with firearms in the years 2001 and 2010, according to the CDC. About two-thirds of the accidental shooting deaths occurred in the owner's home, another 50% occurred in someone else's home. One half of the victims were under age 25. Accidental shootings are usually done by a friend or family member. Many times, it's a brother. Most suicides with guns occur in the home.

Domestic violence involving a gun is more likely to result in a homicide. It is the woman who dies 90% of the time. If there is domestic violence in a home, certainly it would be best if all guns were removed. Some states do that, and others just let it happen, which shows no respect for the woman or her children. What I'm trying to say is if there's a gun in the home, no matter what the circumstance, the most likely person to be injured or killed is someone living in that home. Males are more likely to kill females with a gun by a factor of 5-1.

The US has highly permissive gun laws, and thus faces a far more serious problem with gun violence than other Western nations, as already mentioned. The stark fact is that US children are 13 times more likely to die from firearm homicide, and 18 times more likely to die from a firearm suicide compared to other developed nations. What distinguishes children in the US from children in the rest of the world is the devastating fact that the biggest cause of death in children is firearms.

Let me repeat that because the biggest elephant in the room is gun ownership. I agree that we have the right to own a gun, but that needs to come with education, responsibility, and some measure of mental stability, according to laws that vary from state to state and are difficult to quantify. Mentally unstable people walking around with a gun in their pocket pose a real danger to adults and children. I have noticed essentially nothing has been done since the Las Vegas shootings and the last school shootings. I think the carnage will continue.

Then again, we should be able to control the situation in our own homes. Even with known domestic abuse in the home, I suspect some women will never convince the husband to give up his gun, which puts the whole family at risk, especially the wife and her children.

Guns in the Home

When there are guns in the home, you need to have a conversation with your children about how guns work and why they're not allowed to touch them. Explain to them that firearms are dangerous and that you need to be properly trained to use them. Remind them that kids and teens are killed every day playing with and showing off their guns. It is important that you communicate with your children. If they are under five years of age, find age-appropriate books that explain at their level about gun safety.

Parents have the greatest influence over their children. So, sit down and have an honest conversation about guns. It may save your child's life. If you've had a conversation with them, you still need to secure your gun and put it in a place where they won't have access to it.

If you keep guns unlocked in your bedroom, you're only asking for trouble. Domestic violence is totally unpredictable. Your children can come in, find the gun, play with it, and end up accidentally killing themselves or a brother or sister. Or a neighbor. Or a friend.

The many places *not* to put a gun include:

- on top of the refrigerator.
- under the bed
- behind the couch
- under the mattress
- in the back of the closet
- in the dresser drawer
- in the backyard
- in your purse
- under the seat of the car

Do not ever put a loaded gun in these areas. All it takes is a kid finding the gun and going outside and getting shot or shooting someone.

Here are some additional general gun safety rules:

- Treat all guns as if they are loaded

- Keep a gun pointed in the safest possible direction

- Keep your finger off the trigger until you're ready to shoot

- Know your target, its surroundings, and beyond

- Know how to properly operate your gun

- Never handle a gun when you are angry or depressed

- Never play with a toy replica gun in the street

- Guns should be unloaded when not actually in use

- Store your ammunition in a locked location separate from the firearms

- Remind children if they find an unattended rifle in their home or at a neighbor's home, not to touch it, but to tell an adult.

- Educate everyone in your family about firearm safety. Firearms kept for security reasons should be fully controlled at all times.

- Make sure young people in your home are aware of and understand the safety guidelines concerning firearms.

Harming and Killing Our Children by Allowing Them to Vape

Our children are vaping cigarettes, and, yes, also marijuana. Allowing people to help themselves to nicotine in an attempt to avoid the thousands of chemicals in cigarettes is not the answer to great health for child.

The FDA announced it will give the manufacturers of electronic cigarettes 60 days to prove they can keep e-cigarettes out of the hands of children. Of course, that's an industry lobbying ploy as usual. Money talks. Do you ever feel that our democracy is actually based purely on lobbying money?

Enforcement will not be successful. Industry wins again. It's about the money honey.

The Juul brand of e-cigarettes has different flavors like crème brûlée or cucumber to make them even more irresistible, especially to a child, whose craving for sweets is even higher than an adult's. This has been well tested by the industry. Incidentally, here is something I bet you don't know: there is sugar and cigarettes. Read Dr. Gary Taub's book *The Case against Sugar*. There is a whole chapter devoted to how the industry uses sugar to make cigarettes more addictive. Sugar is what makes the smoke more acidic and opens the alveoli to allow nicotine into the bloodstream. The industry figured that out around 1920 and doubled cigarette sales.

Children are vaping at an increasing rate, especially because of the availability of medical marijuana. The experience in Colorado has not been good. In Indiana, e-cigarettes are now the main source of nicotine among the Indiana youth; 19.7% of Indiana high school students use these cigarettes on a regular basis. Even a higher percentage are smoking marijuana products.

The American Academy of Pediatrics warns that "Juuling" of cigarettes increases addiction, and yet its popularity is booming.

CNBC reported in July that e-cigarette sales have increased 800% in a recent four-week interval this year. Let's face it, if you have one addiction, odds are you will probably have another soon, be it alcohol, marijuana, cigarettes, or sugary food. The Surgeon General of United States has said the addictive potential of e-cigarettes is quite high, and we all know the use of nicotine is very unsafe, especially for children because of their undeveloped brains.

The tobacco industry tried—but fortunately failed—in its effort to win support for e-cigarettes at the World Health Conference in Geneva. Over 137 countries met at the conference in Geneva, Switzerland. The delegates were there for an update on world health related specifically to tobacco. Years ago, the group even formed a treaty to try to control the mental aspect of tobacco and nicotine addiction. A lot of their efforts were somewhat successful, according to reports. But I wondered about that the last time I traveled to Amsterdam. I thought all the people on the street were smoking. Cigarettes and marijuana are sold in their coffee shops. While walking someone rode his bike past me very fast, with a cigarette in his mouth, texting, and no hands on the handlebars. I sure can't ride a bike that well.

Industry has been searching for alternatives to combustible cigarettes because sales are down. Among the devices being considered are e-cigarettes, through which the user inhales flavored nicotine vapors. These chemicals are heated by devices which warm tobacco in a way that supposedly doesn't release carcinogens. Then again, the FDA has not tested these devices for safety. The Juul product is a flash drive look-alike whose popularity has been growing rapidly in America, especially the secondary schools.

Kids are thought to be safer than they would be using traditional cigarettes because they do not get the toxic smoke that comes from tobacco. But little is known about the health effects of all the chemicals they do inhale. Also, there is concern that non-smokers think it's less risky. They could be creating a new generation the smokers. Eventually, they become addicted to the nicotine, that tolerance is increased, maybe setting them on a path to addiction.

Talk to your kids. Don't make a friend out of them. Make them a friend after age 25. Also, of course, set a good example. Two years ago, I visited an elegant couple during a trip to see my cousin. I could not stand to be in that house because the smell of smoke was everywhere. I received a phone call a month ago from my non-smoking cousin that the beautiful couple next door we're both dead from lung cancer.

What's the Answer?

Continuing to do the same thing will not change the outcome.

Harming and killing our children with our thoughtless, addictive, and sometimes even criminal action must stop.

Let's face it, the great majority of us love our children more than anything. We would do whatever we could for them. Animals protect their children with their lives; it is in their genetic structure. But it's maybe not as automatic for us. Many humans lack the necessary knowledge—that's what this book is all about.

The next part contains the most important information of all. I call it *The Call of Life*. It includes 20 prescriptions for a great life for you and your children, the whole family, and the society surrounding you.

If you follow the 20 prescriptions, you'll have a healthy, enjoyable life. They're actually posted throughout Fort Wayne Indiana, in judge's chambers and on a beautiful statue which I paid for in front the Juvenile Justice Center on Wells Street. Stop there on a sunny day, sit on one of the benches, and look at that beautiful statue with the 20 prescriptions written on it.

The Unity Performing Arts Choir for Children has all twenty prescriptions memorized, and you will never meet more happy, singing, dancing and successful kids in one place. They have won national and international acclaim. I am extremely proud of them and their director Marshall White.

CONTENTS *Volume Two*

FOREWORD

I would highly recommend to every parent and child to read and study Dr. Rudy Kachmann's book on character development and good health habits. This whole subject matter came to my attention in the fall of 1999 when I was dining in a favorite local restaurant after a rigorous tennis match with some other worthy opponents. The conversation became very stimulating when we talked about the need for good health habits and character development with our young members of the community and the possibility that this could be taught to them in a school setting or with a formulated curriculum.

At that time, one of the gentlemen present had listed twenty brief sentences covering each of the topics concerning character development, mental and physical health, and challenges to prioritize openness, tolerance, and acceptance in our community, as well as in our personal relations and personal habits. The gentleman who formulated this concept was none other that renowned and skilled neurosurgeon, Rudy Kachmann, M.D., from Fort Wayne, Indiana.

The opportunity to advance these concepts, which we now call the *Twenty Prescriptions for Living the Good Life*, touched me as I listened to the passionate presentation by Dr. Kachmann. He shared his vision of how these principles could be taught to our younger generation and how these principles could possibly change the world. This idea was so stimulating that we continued to meet week after week with the idea of refining these twenty challenges into a cohesive set of "Prescriptions" by which to live and operate one's life.

As an attorney by profession, I was further motivated to pursue researching what laws were legislating these factors in the state of Indiana. I learned that almost all of these behavioral codes were already required to be taught under Indiana Code 20-10.1-4-1 *et seq.*, Mandatory Curriculum, and that public schools in the community have not complied with this law.

Dr. Kachmann had dedicated his professional medical career to saving lives and healing patients and also concentrates his professional medical career to saving lives and healing patients and also concentrates his energies on many of the problems in our community. He is hopeful that the words and concepts in his book will change people's lives for the positive, as well as change everyone around them, so that the *Twenty Prescriptions* become contagious and accepted by all.

Philip R. Terrill J.D.
Attorney at Law
Fort Wayne, Indiana

PREFACE

THE CALL OF LIFE
Appealing for Excellence in Character, Positive Mental and Physical Health Habits and Reconciliation within a Pluralistic Society

My purpose in writing this book is to teach and promote a code of behavior. This code will challenge our communities to develop good character, sound health habits, physically and mentally, and to advance an atmosphere of openness within our communities dominated by pluralism. Tragically, in our nation founded upon freedoms guaranteed by a constitution that includes the separation of church and state, it has been at the expense of the moral fiber of our country. Public schools have lost their voice and no longer speak with conviction in challenging our children's character development. The absence of this voice has left no alternative but to lift up the "Call of Life" in an attempt to fill this void.

It is my sincere belief that subscribing to a moral code, practicing good health habits physically and mentally, and striving to maintain open dialogue will serve to return our society to its intended purpose. My dedication to this "Call of Life" has driven me to place this code of behavior in as many arenas of communication and expression as possible. This code of behavior is entitled, "The Twenty Prescriptions for Living the Good Life." They have been permanently displayed in a dramatic sixteen-foot sculpture that portrays conflict-to-resolution through peaceful coexistence. This sculpture can be seen at the new Juvenile Justice Center in Fort Wayne, Indiana. The "Prescriptions" are also permanently etched on the memorial wall dedicated to the memory of Rev. Jesse White, a leading civil rights activist in my community. It is also exciting to see the "Prescriptions" on the walls of the Fort Wayne Criminal Justice Center. The vocal group known as the "Voices of Unity" has produced the "Twenty Prescriptions" in a variety of creative performing art forms that have been presented at all of their public concerts. It was a privilege to sponsor these talented young children as they traveled throughout Michigan on a tour entitled

"Living the Good Life" where they advanced the "Twenty Prescriptions" each time they performed.

Because of my commitment to youth, I have developed a curriculum for elementary grades one through six. The "Prescriptions" were also a weekly part of the curriculum of Richard Milburn High School, an academic atmosphere for the non-traditional student. I counted it an honor to be this high school's 2004 Commencement speaker. I took great pride in awarding a scholarship to one of the graduates who had written a moving essay that elaborated this individual's personal views of the "Prescriptions." It was a thrill when the Boy Scouts Association had ten counties of Indiana permanently display the "Twenty Prescriptions" of this code of behavior in the main dining hall of their camp located in Angola, Indiana.

Other opportunities for advancement of the "Call of Life" include the new Kachmann Office and Community Center of the NAACP. It was my pleasure to make this facility possible through my contribution to the Urban League. Each individual coming to the offices and utilizing the activity center will come in contact with the "Twenty Prescriptions." The "Prescriptions" will also be an active part of the Public Broadcasting station serving all of northeast Indiana, northwest Ohio and southern Michigan.

We have endeavored to do all that we can to go outside of our local community to advance the "Call of Life." Currently the "Twenty Prescriptions" are being utilized with the young people enrolled in the Star Foundation in Van Wert, Ohio. I am also honored that Florida Gulf Coast University has deemed this code of behavior vital for every incoming freshman. As a result, we are providing the relevant material for all incoming students. I have challenged countless students in schools across the country to read the "Prescriptions" and write, in their own words, what the "Prescriptions" mean to them. Those who have committed themselves to this journey have been rewarded with scholarships to assist them in their preparation for the future.

Enclosed on the cover of the book is a complimentary CD. It is the song that was written and performed by the national recording artist Jeoffrey Benward. I am sure you will be stirred as you listen to the "Call of Life" in a musical interpretation of the "Twenty Prescriptions for Living the Good Life." I would encourage you to compare the words that Mr. Benward wrote with the words of the "Twenty Prescriptions" as I believe it will make the song even more meaningful.

The purpose of including these efforts and activities is to express what one individual's commitment can do to make a difference. It is my hope that you will hear the "Call of Life" as you read the pages of this book and listen to the movingly beautiful song. I am sure "The Call" will stir you to action, and all of us together can raise a voice to carry the message to our next generation. If you would like to contact me, please feel free to use the web site, mailing address, or telephone number that is enclosed.

Dr. Rudy Kachmann, MD

INTRODUCTION

Fame is fleeting, popularity an accident; riches take wings. Only one thing endures: character.

Horace Greeley

Intelligence plus character—that is the goal of true education.

Martin Luther King, Jr.

What can I contribute to help prevent the moral bankruptcy of the next generation? It is impossible to escape the urgency of this impeding question. As we are confronted daily with Martha Stewart verdicts of "guilty," and disclosures of corporate scandals like Enron, we have to wonder what moral heritage we are leaving our children. I was disheartened to read an October 30, 2002-*USA Today* article, "Parents Feel They're Failing to Teach Values":

> Parents don't believe they are doing a very good job teaching their kids essential values. Across the board, from teaching kids self-discipline to basic manners, parents give themselves very low grades, according to a new study from Public Agenda, a nonprofit organization.
>
> Though 83% of parents say it is vital to teach kids self-control, only 34% say that they have succeeded. And although 82% of adults believe it is essential to teach their children to do their best in school, only 50% say they have gotten the message across. Parents believe they are swimming upstream against a strong current of harmful messages to children.

These statements convinced me that we must do all we can to help the next generation know the importance that values will play in their lives. The *USA Today* article cited a national survey of 1,607 parents of children ages 5-17 assessing how effectively essential character values were being taught to their children. Regardless of the families' income, location or other demographic measures, the results were similar:

Good money habits: 50% say this is an essential value
28% say they taught them to their children

Honesty:	91% call it an essential value
	55% feel they have succeeded in teaching it
Courtesy:	84% believe it is an essential value
	62% think they have succeeded in teaching it

In conclusion, the same survey expressed the following parents' fears for their kids:

79%—protecting their child from drugs and alcohol
76%—the negative influences of other kids on their child
73%—negative messages in the media

Compelling information like this inspired me to try to make a difference. In my search for solutions, I sought many resources, including the philosophy of St. Thomas Aquinas, who examines the four cardinal virtues of prudence, justice, temperance, and fortitude in his *Summa Theologica.* He thought these virtues were not an end in themselves, but a *means to the highest end.* The Greeks expounded on strong character as a result of the four virtues of *wisdom*, lived out through good judgment; *justice*, which is respecting the rights of all persons; *fortitude*, or the ability to do what is right in the face of difficulty; and *self-control.*

More contemporary authors, such as Peter Gomes, who wrote *The Good Life (Truths That Last in Time Or Need)*, provide thought-provoking insights into discovering the paths of virtue. One author in particular made an indelible impression upon me as someone offering a positive alternative to cultivate the human spirit—-Thomas Lickona. Lickona expands these virtues of antiquity to include *love* and all it encompasses; a *positive attitude*, which is such a small thing that makes a big difference; *hard work* involving personal initiative, diligence, goal-setting, and resourcefulness; *integrity*, or telling the truth to oneself; *gratitude*, the secret to a happy life; and *humility*, which is the foundation of moral life.

The question you may ask as a reader is, "What qualifies you to address these concerns?" That is a question I have asked myself. For more than 35 years, it has been my privilege to serve my community as a neurosurgeon. My profession affords me the unique privilege of dealing with patients and family members from every walk of life. It is my belief that I am to treat the whole person—mind, body, soul and spirit. Those whom I have cared for often needed much more than physical recovery. As I interacted with my patients, fellow doctors, nurses, and other professionals across the country, a code of behavior began to evolve through our discussions. These principles impressed me so much that I began writing them down, and found myself sharing them, and challenging others to make a commitment with me to strive to live them. This code of behavior has become known as "Dr. Kachmann's Prescriptions for Living the Good Life." I am honored that others identified these with my name, and accepted the challenge to apply the "Twenty Prescriptions" to their lives. My passion to make a difference led me to advance these "Prescriptions" through many unique venues. My primary qualification is my motivating desire to help parents, teachers, and society to produce young adults that will make a difference in our world.

With this, I dedicate my book to the following:

All the people over the past 35 years who have willingly dialogued with me about these "Prescriptions," helping me to formulate this code of behavior.

To my children whom I love unconditionally, and hope will follow the "Prescriptions" and teach them to my grandchildren.

To my darling wife, Rhonda, who has graciously hosted so many events that have contributed to the advancement of this program. She unselfishly stands by me in our donation of all our resources to make a difference.

I also want to express my thanks to all the insights so freely shared by those whom I asked to be a part of this book, and I know every reader will benefit from their contribution.

Dr. Rudy Kachmann, MD

Rx One

TREAT OTHERS AS YOU WOULD LIKE TO BE TREATED.

I set out to find a friend, but couldn't find one. I set out to be a friend, and friends were everywhere.

—Anonymous

Kindness begets kindness.

—Sophocles

July of 1969 was an eventful time of my life. I had to decide where I would settle down and establish my surgical practice. My affection for the state of Indiana was long-standing since my years of undergraduate work and medical school at Indiana University. I had made many friends and enjoyed a variety of pleasant experiences, especially fishing in the beautiful freshwater lakes of northern Indiana. They were peaceful encounters with nature and a rejuvenation of mind, body, and soul, as well as the delight in the "catch of the day."

I entered into a partnership with another doctor that was a bright start for establishing my neurosurgical practice. To finally be doing what I had been preparing for all of my life was a thrilling prospect. The first six months were challenging and the work was demanding, but all of this was fulfilling, and it seemed that my new life in Indiana was coming together. I also secured my first mortgage on a home for my family. All the demanding years of sacrifice through medical school, internship, and residency now seemed well worth it.

My family's first Christmas in Fort Wayne was now upon us, and the joy of the season filled our home. The children and my wife were filled with the thrill of giving and receiving presents. There was great satisfaction from watching them enjoy the holiday. Despite the fact that my credit cards had reached their limits, I had confidence that those obligations would be fulfilled with the New Year's schedule.

New Year's Eve of 1969 will be a night forever etched in my memory. My wife and I were dressing for the evening, anticipating our first New Year's Eve party as part of the Fort Wayne community. The memory of that night is very vivid, even as I recall it now. While putting the finishing touches on my tuxedo, looking forward to the activities of the evening ahead, I was distracted by the sound of the doorbell. What an unexpected surprise when I opened the door and saw standing there my neurosurgical partner. As the snow was falling in the wintry cold, I invited my partner to come into my home. I did my best to contain my excitement as I presumed his presence suggested a year-end bonus as a result of the success of my performance in the first six months of practice. He said he could only stay for a moment, and had something he needed to drop off. I graciously extended my hands to receive the box and envelope he was holding. I will never forget the horror of discovering that the envelope—far from containing a bonus—was a letter stating my dismissal! The box contained the contents from my office. The final words before his departure were that the locks of the offices had been changed, and it would not be necessary for me to return.

The walk upstairs to my wife was one of the longest walks of my life. My mind raced with the thoughts: How was I going to explain my termination to my family? How was I going to pay for the Christmas season we had just enjoyed? How was I going to meet the next mortgage payment? I decided not to spoil the New Year's Eve holiday for my wife and small children. Suppressing the heartbreak of this evening's dreadful news, I made every effort for that night to be one of celebration, even though the outlook for the New Year was a bleak one.

Not only was I without a medical office and staff, I did not even have any surgical instruments at my disposal. I will always remember my dear friend, Dr. Scheeringa who came to me, heavy-hearted upon hearing of my dismissal, and offered his office space and surgical equipment at no charge. I don't know what I would have done without friends like this.

Just as there seemed to be a ray of hope, another devastating experience transpired in my life. I received a letter from an attorney representing my former practice. (Let me pause here to explain that a common practice among doctors is for them to write off the difference between what a patient owes for medical services, and what their insurance company will pay. This is done at the doctor's discretion based on his personal conviction that the patient would be unable to meet the financial responsibility, and would only be an added pressure on their family's financial situation.) I had extended this kindness to several of my patients who were in need. Now I stood reading a letter threatening legal action if I didn't pay back all of those differences to my former partner. My heart almost stopped as I had more than $30,000 added to my financial burdens.

It was at this time that I made sincere resolves for my life. These events could either have been stumbling blocks that would have resulted in bitterness and anger, or building blocks to develop the character needed to rebuild my career. I chose the latter. Within a year, through hard work and determination, I was blessed with a promising neurosurgical practice, and I finally had the resources to meet all of my financial obligations. These life-changing experiences led me to resolve to "treat others as I would like to be treated."

As a doctor, I deal daily with a diversity of people under a variety of stressful circumstances, including patients facing life-threatening injuries and surgeries. I also attend to patients who are rushed into the emergency room suffering from trauma as a result of some tragic accident. There are those painful times when I must go to the family members who are anxiously waiting for word of their loved ones only to be told—"I'm sorry, but we did all we could do,they are gone." My experience over the past 35 years is that people confronting devastating circumstances respond to kindness and courtesy rather than cold, clinical professionalism. Anyone who wants to be successful in dealing with people, whether in the medical profession or any other job setting, needs to adopt the Prescription: treat others as you would like to be treated.

Whatever success I may have achieved in the medical profession can be attributed to a driving desire to make a positive difference in people's lives. Each day I approach a patient in the office for a consultation, or in their hospital room as I make rounds, or just before they are wheeled into surgery—I take this first prescription to heart. I try to treat my patients and their families as I would like to be treated if I were in their place.

When talking with others from a variety of backgrounds in preparation for this book, I found a common theme. No matter what their occupation, they all seemed to attribute one act as the key to attaining their status; they believed that kind and courteous treatment of others has ultimately made them who they are in life. My friend, and former patient, Sheriff Oates Archey of Grant County, Indiana observed, after reviewing the "Twenty Prescriptions", that if this one isn't the first, none of the others will have any substance.

As a sheriff who deals with some of the most challenging individuals in society, he could choose to take a hard approach, yet Sheriff Archey seeks to treat criminals and prisoners as he would want to be treated. He told me this Prescription is the motive that drives the actions of all the other Prescriptions. Sheriff Archey seeks to apply it, not only with the prisoners, but also in his daily interactions with his staff and sheriff's deputies. I am certain that this strong character trait is the reason Grant County has re-elected Sheriff Archey. Kind treatment of others and courteous acts throughout his life have made this gracious man one that prisoners and community members alike hold in high esteem.

Another person I found to be committed to this Prescription in a challenging environment is the Honorable William C. Lee, a U.S. District Court Judge. Every day Judge Lee deals with attorneys, jurors, and defendants whose lives could be affected forever by the verdict he decrees. Judge Lee believes that a large part of being the best judge is applying the Golden Rule; to do unto others as you would want others to do unto you. Any of us standing before a judge assuredly would be grateful to know this is a motivation in his heart as he renders decisions that can significantly impact our lives.

"Courtesy" evolves from the root word "court." In Western civilization the elite organizations were the courts of the kings and queens. The members of royal courts behaved with a formal elegance and dignity that exceeded the customs of the average person of that time. The standards for manners and fine dining developed into the Codes for Etiquette, or the rules for "courtliness" and "courtesy."

In modern American society, although we are not governed by monarchs or restricted from the "courts" of the elite, we can subscribe to the "royal" way of living—we can be "courteous" in our lives.

Holding a door for another, driving courteously, and habitually using words like "please," and "thank you" promotes an atmosphere of courtesy.

Many of my friends who have successful marriages and happy families believe random acts of kindness are the glue that holds their home together. It's kind to leave a bathroom the way you find it. Kindness is expressed in so many ways and really doesn't require expending much energy.

I am convinced that character has many components, but there are four that stand out to me: 1) choices we make; 2) values we embrace; 3) crises we endure; 4) associates we keep.

The challenge of the first Prescription is to make choices daily to be kind and courteous to others. Hold "treating others as you would like to be treated" as a valuable trait to cultivate in life. Even when your circumstances may be out of your authority to control. Let kindness be your choice. Associate with people who will be an example and encourage you in your pursuit. Determine to respond to others the way you would like them to respond to you.

Constant kindness can accomplish much. As the sun makes the ice melt, kindness causes misunderstanding, mistrust and hostility to evaporate.

—Albert Schweitzer

Rx Two

BE HONEST; DO NOT LIE, CHEAT OR STEAL—MAKE YOUR WORD YOUR BOND.

Honesty is the first chapter in the book of wisdom.
—Thomas Jefferson

Never esteem anything as of advantage to thee that shall make thee break thy word or loose thy self-respect.
—Marcus Ayrelius

A gentleman is one who keeps his promises to those who cannot enforce them.
—Anonymous

Another interesting story appeared in an article in *USA Today*. The Board of Directors at Bausch & Lomb decided to withhold a 1.1 million-dollar bonus from their CEO rather than accept his resignation for lying on his resume. The executive claimed that he had graduated from a prestigious business school in 1978; the truth was that he had attended the school from 1973-1976, but left without graduating. Not only was this a great financial loss for the chief executive officer, but also, I am sure, a tremendous embarrassment for him and his family. The real tragedy is that apparently the company believed in this man's abilities or they would have accepted his resignation. Instead, he had to bear the shame of misrepresenting the truth for perceived personal advantage.

The American corporate culture has another recent example to illustrate the vital importance of the second prescription. Martha Stewart is a woman who commanded respect as she turned a small home catering business into a billion-dollar dynasty. Home entertainment evolved into an entirely new dimension because of Stewart's powerful drive and influence. Many sat in total shock as the news reported that her empire would be marred, if not destroyed, as a result of one tragic character flaw; Stewart was found guilty of not telling the truth. What better example could we have as a society that the prescription of honesty is required at every level, even at the top.

While working with various judges over the years, I observed a common thread that was woven into the fabric of their character. One judge's comments in particular stood out to me. Judge Steven Sims told me that commitment to the second Prescription would help avoid considerable stress and anxiety in life, as well as contribute to a successful life. Unquestionably, as a judge, he has witnessed many lives destroyed because of lying, cheating and stealing.

I read an interesting story about J. Edgar Hoover, the renowned FBI Director; when asked, "What would you tell a son?", he replied:

> *Above all, I would teach him to tell the truth. Truth-telling, I have found, is the key to a responsible citizenship. The thousands of criminals I have seen in 40 years of law enforcement have had one thing in common; every single one was a liar.*

In my practice of medicine, I have found that trust is the most critical relationship a patient must have with their doctor. Trust can never be attained without a foundation of honesty. An individual may have a good education and the best of skills, blessed with gifts; but his or her career is doomed if no one can respect their word. Respect is cultivated in a field of trust. In my profession, a patient ultimately trusts their life to me. My patients must be able to trust that I told them the truth regarding their need for surgery. That trust and respect gives them the confidence to fare a potentially life-threatening procedure despite their uncertainty. If they respect my truthfulness and believe in my skills, they will entrust their life in my hands.

Honesty and a willingness to admit when we are wrong are the only ways to promote personal growth, and to further advance your profession. Honesty is the foundation for all relationships. As a doctor, I have spent a considerable number of years in schooling and in an educational environment. The temptation to cheat and take the road of less work was always there. As I look back now, I realize that had I yielded to those temptations, I would never have gained the knowledge I need to perform my duties as a neurosurgeon today. Nevertheless, as I reflect on cheating, the significance goes much deeper.

The motivation to cheat is not only a short cut from long hours of studying and preparation; behind cheating is a desire for recognition of accomplishment. In assuming that an "unearned" good grade will result in satisfaction and self-esteem, the student compromises his or her character. The end result is the opposite. The cheater has to live with the longer-lasting and deeper loss of self-respect and dignity. William Shakespeare once said, "If I loose my honor, I loose myself." The great American writer, Ralph Waldo Emerson also observed, "A little integrity is better than my career."

In my introduction, I shared that I am committed to treatment of the whole person. Much will be said in the following chapters regarding the care of the body and the development of the mind. Intertwined in the fabric of the prescriptions is deep belief in the spirituality of humankind. I don't seek to impose my definitions of spirituality—nor is this book an attempt to establish any particular concept of a "Higher Being." However, I believe that a lack of commitment to truthfulness, and to choose to cheat or steal and not to make your word our bond, will result in the diminishing quality of anyone's spiritual life.

Honesty is central to my faith.

—Judge Charles F. Pratt

This prescription was instilled in me by my parents. I was always told to be honest and truthful and good things will come to you. God smiles on those who live right.

—Sheriff Oates Archey

℞ Three

TREAT LIFE WITH CARE; AVOID RISKY BEHAVIOR.

Courage is almost a contradiction in terms. It means a strong desire to live, taking the form of readiness to die.

—G. K. Chesterton

Courage is resistance to fear, mastery of fear–not absence of fear. Except a creature be part coward it is not a compliment to say it is brave.

—Mark Twain

The quotes above may seem like unusual maxims to begin the Third Prescription, but hopefully it will become clear why I have selected statements about courage when avoiding undue risks. I was privileged to serve my country as an officer in the US Navy during the Vietnam War. As a neurosurgeon, I witnessed and attended to many young soldiers with serious injuries. Today we are witnessing soldiers returning from Iraq with injuries that they will carry for the rest of their lives; wounds that were the result of the risk they took to bring forth liberty for the citizens of Iraq. I want to commend the risks that our brave soldiers have taken along with the courage exhibited by the soldiers of our coalition. Their sacrifices were surely coupled with intense fears that had to be faced and conquered in order to pursue a greater good.

This is the challenge: convincing youth that they are not invincible and to treat life with care by avoiding undue risks. First you must understand that I deal daily with people who have been rushed to the Emergency Room. Their brains and the potential to think, create and imagine may never again function with propensity because a helmet was overlooked and a risk was taken. Legs will never again be used for running, dancing, or even to walk; arms that could have hugged and held; fingers that would have written poems, drawn sketches, painted pictures, and played musical instruments will never again function because a seat belt was not worn; or a reckless dive into shallow water snaps a neck, and now I stand with a family who will have to care for their loved one for the rest of their lives.

While writing this book, a very unfortunate accident took place. A young man in the prime of his life, named Noel, was standing on the flat bed of a pick up truck. It was certainly a risky choice and that careless moment resulted in a lifetime of grave adversity. Young Noel was flipped from the truck and landed headfirst on the ground resulting in a tragic brain injury. I am pleased to say that Noel is making great progress in his rehabilitation, and will be able to participate in the Wheel Chair Athletic Foundation that I have established in the Tri-State area, for just such unfortunate men and women. I am reminded, each time I see Noel in an office visit, of the importance of life being treated with care, and that risky behavior must be avoided.

For as long as I can remember in my medical practice, deaths have occurred because:

- Drugs and alcohol were abused.
- Seatbelts were not fastened (more than one-half of the young drivers killed in car accidents were not wearing seatbelts).
- Motorcycles were recklessly ridden.
- Guns were not protected from children, or used violently in an argument.
- Wave runners were used without careful instructions being followed.

Every day of my practice I have to stand with grieving families who have lost a father, mother, son, or daughter. If they aren't grief-stricken over a loss by death, they are facing the permanent disability of a once active member of their home.

An October 19, 2003 *Parade* magazine article gave a staggering statistic:

> Eight children or teenagers are killed by firearms each day. An American child is twelve times more likely to die from gunfire than a child in any other industrialized nation.

Certainly we should not be thwarted from approaching our vast reservoirs of potential because the roads are guarded by dragons of fear. Fear has barred far too many from enjoying life, causing them to miss experiences that could enhance the quality of their lives. Most definitely we stand in appreciation for risks taken with courage, in the midst of fear, by our sons and daughters in times of war. I acknowledge that each time I sit behind the wheel of a car I am taking a risk, and that fear must be conquered or I would never leave home. But I treat life with care by fastening my seatbelt, obeying traffic laws, shutting off the cell phone, and driving as defensively as possible.

As Mark Twain said, "We need to have courage to face, resist, and master our fears."I do not believe that this is best illustrated by MTV's program "Jackass," which challenges people to perform stunts that could maim them for life. The network reality show, "Fear Factor" is not instilling courage in our lives either, but rather distorting our value of our most treasured possession—the gift of life. This gift is far too precious to risk it with dangerous choices. It is my sincere belief that the mind is clouded and good choices obscured when it is affected by the destructive influence of alcohol and drugs. More on this will be discussed later in the book, but this Prescription could not be fairly presented without exposing the reality of the dangers that substance abuse has on the careless disregard for life in making choices that involve risky behavior.

Rx Four

PRACTICE SHOWING RESPECT FOR AUTHORITY; PARENTS, TEACHERS, POLICE, AND GOVERNMENT.

Without feelings of respect, what is there to distinguish man from beasts?
—Confucius

He that respects not, is not respected.
—George Herbert

If you have some respect for people as they are, you can be more effective in helping them to become better than they are.
—John W. Garner

Each summer, one of the greatest sources of relaxation for my wife and me is to spend time at our lake cottage. It is a chance to get away from the pressures and responsibilities, and enjoy a beautiful, different environment. It is always a special pleasure when we are able to share this experience with friends and family. This was particularly the case during the summer I wrote this book.

Rhonda is such a gracious hostess and generously provides for our guests. One weekend, she invited her brother, who had grown up with her in the lake region where our cottage is located. They invited some of their childhood friends over, who in turn, asked if they could bring their children. The children had boyfriends and girlfriends who also came over to our cottage. Before we knew it, Rhonda was performing the "multiplication of fish and loaves" of Biblical proportions! (My wife never ceases to amaze me—how can she pull off such astonishing feasts at the spur of the moment!) I looked over the serene landscape and saw more than twenty people I had never met before in my life, and was beginning to wonder if word was spreading–"Dinner at Kachmann's! Come on! Let's go!"

One outstanding thing struck me on this occasion and came as a pleasant surprise. Everyone was very polite and sought to help out in any way possible. Before using the wave runner or any sports equipment, permission was always asked. When our evening meal ended and the time of sharing ceased, everyone rose to their feet as if on cue. Plates were removed and washed, pots and pans were cleaned, and the grill and tables were scrubbed. All was restored so that you never knew there had been a meal. Throughout the entire day, there were words expressed that aren't often heard today. "Yes sir," or "Yes Ma'am," "please," and "thank you." What could have been a day that never ended, became a day that was sad to close. It made quite an impression on me and will be long remembered.

What made a difference that day? It was a simple word, "respect." The guests that day showed respect to my wife and me, and our home. As a result, I found myself respecting all of them. I respected the parents who obviously had modeled, in raising their children, how to respect authority. I suppose that is why I like the quote at the beginning of this chapter of George Herbert:

He that respects not is not respected.

Sometimes we are disillusioned with our families, and parents in particular, are subjects of criticism. Because of this disillusionment, many children find grounds, in their minds, not to honor parental authority. Steven R. Covey, a New York Times best-selling author, in *The 7 Habits of Highly Effective Families*, devotes an entire chapter to a very interesting observation on pages 9-10:

> Good families–even great families–are off track 90% of the time! The key is they have a sense of destination. They know what the 'track' looks like. And they keep coming back to it time and time again.

Mr. Covey uses this metaphor throughout his book, and it clearly helps make his point. We don't just respect those who are "perfect," but those who make mistakes, and get back on course.

The word respect is derived from the Latin word "spicere," meaning, "to look." It is the same root word of "spectacles"–lenses that allow the wearer not only to look, but to actually see things of importance if we are alert. We are not always alert. Sometimes in order to show respect, we need to look beyond the surface and allow the lenses of our character to see what can be respected.

Find something that can be respected in the authority figures of our lives. For example, do not dwell on the negatives of certain teachers, but look for a good quality. Rather than dwell on one police officer who abused his authority, "look" at all the others who put their lives on the line everyday for our safety. Sheriff Archey reflected, "I have shown respect to positions of authority, and now that I sit in a position of authority, respect is shown to me."

One of the great joys I derive from providing the Kachmann Auditorium in the Lutheran Hospital in Fort Wayne, Indiana is that it is used for seminars furthering educational advancement. One such experience took place with the young adults from the inner city of Fort Wayne. These young people are under the direction of Rev. Michael Latham, President of the local chapter of the NAACP.

I served as one of the speakers along with our local sheriff and the assistant Prosecutor of Allen County. I was asked to speak on the "Twenty Prescriptions" and their relevance to these young adults in their endeavor to receive employment, and to equip themselves to improve the quality of their lives. Many of these young people have had multiple uncomfortable experiences with authority figures—particularly with law enforcement officers.

The sheriff and the prosecutor spoke to my heart as they strongly emphasized the importance of showing respect for police officers, and how it can change the outcome in stressful situations.

What an important benefit will be ours if we take this Prescription to heart! Someday, you may be a parent; perhaps you will be a teacher or police officer, or in a position at your job where people answer to you. As Sheriff Archey noted, because he learned to respect authority, that respect is now given to him. Even if we cannot respect a certain individual, "look" beyond the person, and "see" the institution that person represents, and show respect.

℞

Five

DO NOT LET PHYSICAL OR MENTAL ABUSE GO UNNOTICED.

If you sin by not stepping up and offering yourself as a witness to something you've heard or seen in cases of wrongdoing, you'll be held responsible.

—Leviticus 5:1 (The Message)

It is better to protest than to accept injustice.

—Rosa Parks

He injures the good who spares the bad.

—Publius Syrys

Most of my career has been spent in law enforcement and I am a big advocate for reporting and ceasing violence.

—Oates Archey, Sheriff, Grant County, Indiana

Early in my practice I was called to attend a patient that would affect my life deeply; a small infant in the hospital Emergency Room. His father had beaten him. The baby's injuries were substantial. Trauma to the head resulted in blindness. He would never speak or walk. A tracheostomy would be his only means of taking a breath for the rest of his life. This precious infant would never grow up to play on playgrounds, read a storybook, or sing a song. He would spend the little life he had left in a state-funded nursing home. The tragedy is that his mother stood by as the father released his twisted frustrations on the defenseless child.

Often I will see cases where women have been so severely beaten that there is only so much brain surgery can restore. Sadly, almost one million cases of children in our community are victims of domestic violence and treated in our hospitals each year.

My heart was broken to hear the story of a student at a local high school where our Prescriptions are taught. He is a handsome young man who, like many today, enjoys wearing articles of jewelry. When asked about the big silver cross he wore, noticeably repaired, he responded, " I wear it to protect myself when my Dad hits me. That's why I had to get it fixed." When his story was pursued a little farther, we discovered that his uncle paid to have it fixed. Maybe the uncle should have dealt with repairing the *father* who had hit his son so hard it broke a piece of *jewelry!*

I am blessed to still have with me in life, my precious mother. Because of my German heritage, her name is "Oma." Much will be said later in my book about growing up, and the role my "Oma" played in my life. Today she is 96 years old. She is best taken care of, because of her needs, in a fine nursing home in our community. My wife and I cared for her at home until it was necessary, for her well being, to move her to this caring facility. Every week I go and spend time with her. As I drive away, I am always reminded that while she has a warm environment with proper care, others are less fortunate.

Elder abuse and neglect is one of the greatest "hidden crimes" in our culture today. Many elder citizens spend their last years unattended to the point that they are not even bathed for months. They also suffer from improper nutrition, if they are fed at all–to say *nothing* of the filthy environments where they are forced to live. Many times their social security checks are improperly and illegally taken by family or "friends" under pretense of looking out for the elder's best interests.

It is my hope that we will all take a good dose of the Fifth Prescription: "Do not let physical or mental abuse go unnoticed." When we become aware of a child, elderly adult or any other victim of abuse, do not say, "Am I my brother's keeper?" I've always appreciated the noted psychiatrist, Dr. Paul Kapper's response:

> *The answer to the question, "Am I my brother's keeper?" must always be, "No! I am my brother's brother!"*

We must be willing to stand up to abuse in our society. I once read a Chinese proverb that said, "It is better to light a candle than to curse the darkness." It is easy to complain about the horrible things that happen to others; it is another thing to say, "I will report this." John F. Kennedy made a profound statement:

> *Our most basic common link is that we all inhabit this planet. We all breathe the same air. We all cherish our children's future. And we're all moral.*

We must demonstrate that we are "moral" by including, "If I do nothing to help, nothing will get done." Perhaps there is concern that names will be revealed if a report is made of domestic violence or elder abuse. The Mental Health Association's policy is to unconditionally protect the anonymity of every caller.

> *Love cannot remain by itself—it has no meaning. Love has to be put into action, and that action is service.*
>
> —Mother Teresa

Songs can be sung and speeches delivered about love and caring, but we must put love into action through service. There is no greater service we can do than reporting abuse of another. If you're a student, have courage to tell a teacher. If you're a neighbor, it is as simple as a phone call to the local Mental Health Association or a 911 call.

Americans sat in horror during the winter of 2004 as we watched the videotaped abduction of Carrie Bruscia in Sarasota, Florida. The kidnaping from the car wash parking lot epitomizes the fear of every parent. I would like to introduce an article from MSNBC TV offering advice from a former FBI agent on how to keep your children protected from strangers:

> The abduction of 11 year old Carrie Bruscia is every parents' nightmare—you're not there, even for a moment, and a stranger approaches your child, would your child know what to do? There are some precautions you can take as a parent, and information and skills you can teach your child to prevent abduction. Former FBI agent Clint Van Zandt lectures on child and family safety, and offers the following tips to keep

your child out of harm's way:

1. Do not get into a car unless your parents tell you to do it.
2. Stay away from anyone who follows you on foot or in a car. You do not need to go near a car to talk to people inside.
3. Grown ups and other people who need help should not be asking children for help; they should be asking older people.
4. Grown ups should not be asking you for directions, or to look for a "lost puppy", or telling you that your mother or father is in trouble and that they will take you to them.
5. Quickly get away from anyone who tries to take you somewhere and yell and scream, "This man (or woman) is trying to take me away!" or "This is not my father (or mother)!"
6. You should use the buddy system and never go places alone.
7. Always ask your parent's permission to leave the yard or play area, or go into someone's house.
8. Never hitchhike or try to get a ride with someone unless your parents have told you it is OK to ride with them.
9. People should not ask you to keep a special secret. If they do, tell your parents or teacher.
10. Tell anyone who wants to take your picture, "NO!", and tell your parents or teacher.
11. No one should touch you on parts of your body covered by your bathing suit, nor should you touch anyone else in those areas.
12. You can be assertive, and you have the right to say, "NO!" to someone, including adults, and even relatives or friends who try to take you somewhere, touch you, or make you feel uncomfortable in any way.

Many parents use a special code word that only the child knows to convey a message should someone other than a parent ask a child to accompany them anywhere. You can have your child practice a special yell. It is low, loud, and long. It tells the person trying to hurt the child, "I know what to do! I'm not an easy victim!" It tells everyone within the sound of the child's voice, "I need help!" It gets the child going and breaks the spell. A child should not panic and freeze thereby becoming immobile in an emergency. When you yell, you take a deep breath, thereby getting oxygen and energy to your brain and muscles. A child's yell can give him (or her) courage to get their feet moving and to run away.

A Las Vegas, Nevada television station, KVBC-TV, ran the following story, February 6, 2004, with the challenge to make it every community's local news. I hope it will benefit every reader, particularly parents of school-age children:

Vegas School Kids Learn About Stranger Dangers

A lot of people are now wondering, what did Carrie's abductor say to get her to cooperate? Unfortunately, predators can use any number of tricks to lure a child away.

News 3's Denise Roach reports some local kids are learning, not all strangers appear mean.

This was an assembly planned long before the kidnapping in Florida. Members of the Nevada Youth Alliance are showing kids how to protect themselves, and how bad people don't always look like monsters.

"I'm sorry, I can't hear you, can you come closer to the van?" It's called the "ABCs of Tricks." It's a short movie reminding kids to be careful around strangers. At Kermit Booker Elementary School, it's a message being taught to kids as young as three. "That's why we don't let you walk alone."

This week the nation watched in horror as a surveillance camera recorded some of the final moments of an 11-year-old girl's life, as she was led away by a man police say eventually killed her. David Osman, with Nevada Youth Alliance tells kids, "No matter what a stranger says, do not go with them!" Some think they have to look a certain way.

Osman says predators are also known to tell children there's a family emergency and their mom or dad has sent the stranger to get the child. Osman says parents should create a code word so their kids will know when to trust and when to run. Fourth grader, Arteon Ewell says it happened to him, "I ran into the house!"

"I dub thee, Sir Cook. Keep the children safe at Booker."

To help the kids remember, Osman also introduces a little fun, knighting teachers, and sharing a pledge to keep themselves safe. "And to look out for all their friends at Booker Elementary."

Booker Elementary also has a Law Enforcement Club, sponsored by the FBI. Kids learn about all aspects of law enforcement, including these safety tips. Club members helped arrange this assembly so all kids at Booker will be safe.

Nevada Youth Alliance provides many of their safety kits free of charge.

PHOTOGRAPHS

Reading, studying, helping patients, people, and communities.

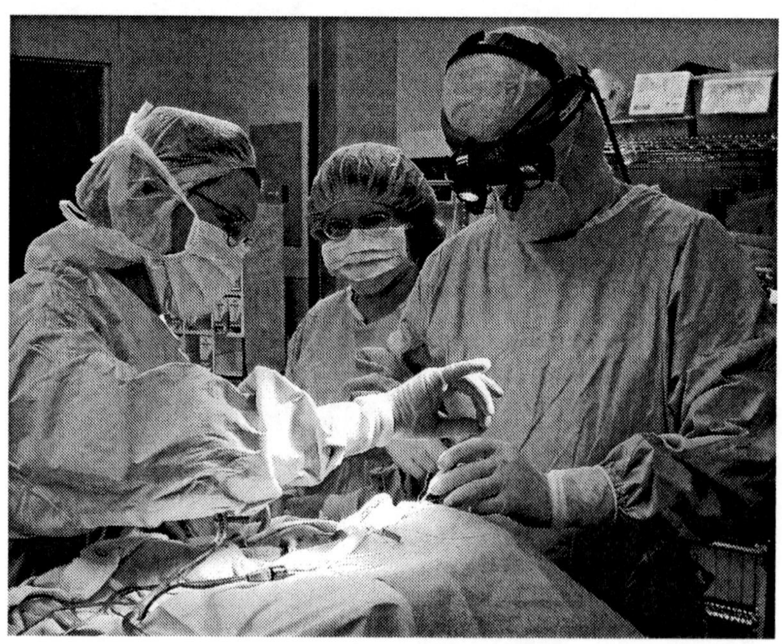

Dr. Kachmann, Neurosurgeon

Lecturing at the Kachmann Auditorium

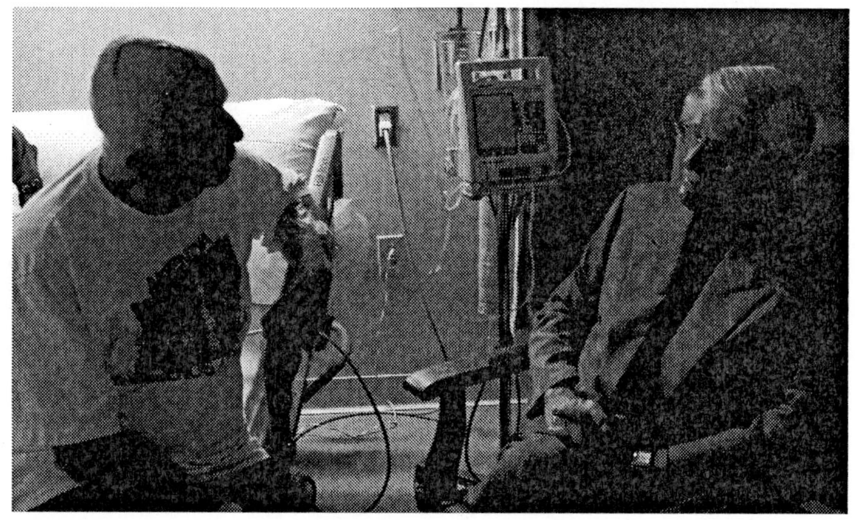

Talking with patients

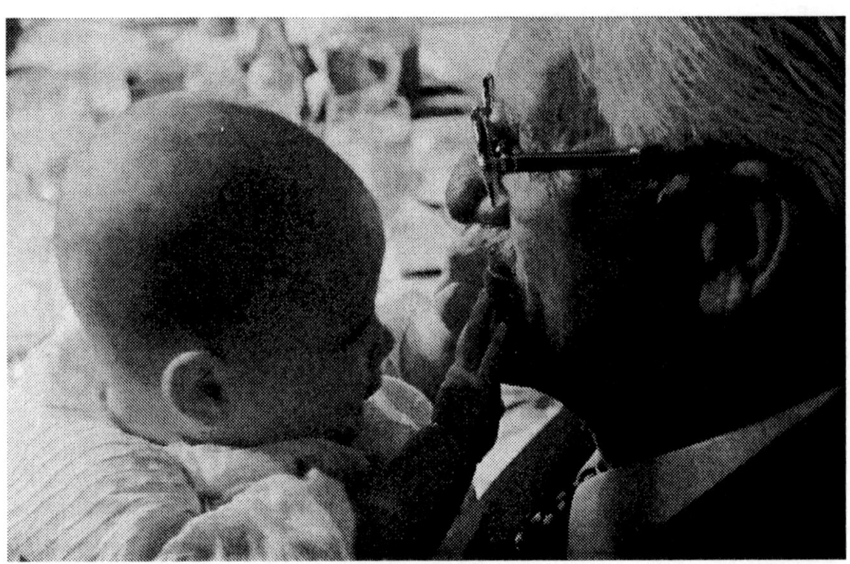

Loving Grandparent

Dedicated to medicine

A special award for a special man

Studying nature

Let's play baseball

Helping children

An honor to receive the Martin Luther King, Jr. Award

Childhood in Germany

New Years 2000: Beginning a new century of hope

Music at Carnegie Hall; New York, New York

Father Daughter Day at Indiana University

Relaxing (fishing and kyaking all in one)

Queen's Theatre in London: Tribute to Fred Astaire Event

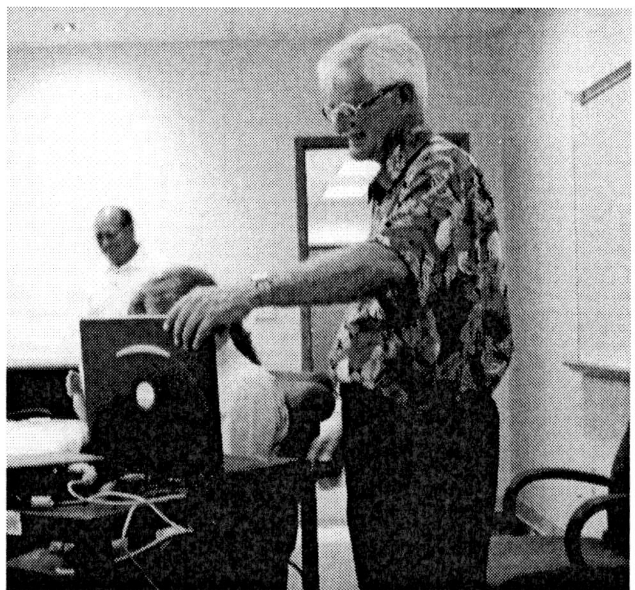

Lecturing at Florida Gulf Coast University

Young man in Germany (looking to his future)

Resting

Having fun with family

Being a Philanthropist

Andre Rieu and Mrs. Kachmann

Working with artist Garcia on sculpture

Childhood with mother

Playing in Carnegie Hall

Champion Senior Tennis Player

Dr. Kachmann in the kitchen

Andre Rieu and Dr. Kachmann's 96 year old mother Auguste Kachmann

Andre Rieu concert

℞ Six

READ A BOOK—REGULARLY.

For the previous chapters I have introduced the Prescription by using various quotes that I thought were relevant to the topic. This prescription reminds me of an often used quote, but I have no idea who originated it.

Good things come in small packages.

This quote may seem a little peculiar at first in relation to this Prescription's challenge, but let me explain why I have chosen it.

The Sixth Prescription has only four words, making it the shortest of the "Twenty Prescriptions for Living the Good Life". Though few in words, it has the potential to provide "good things" for all who practice what it says. My life's course was strongly influenced by a book my mother gave me as a child. It was written by a doctor, and it was about his personal experiences as a physician. I knew then that I wanted to be a doctor. Despite all the boyhood activities and distractions that could have motivated me, like basketball and tennis, I knew that medicine was what I wanted to study and make my profession. Over the years, reading has been a source of joy; I directly attribute any expansion of my intellect to the discipline and pleasure of reading.

There is another judge in Fort Wayne whom I hold in great respect. The Honorable Charles T. Pratt not only brings dignity to the bench as he presides with a sense of fairness and justice, but outside the courtroom he directs his energies to worthwhile activities. One of his greatest passions is reading. He believes there is a direct correlation between the inability to read and lack of reading, and the amount of juvenile crime that exists in our communities. Because of this conviction, Judge Pratt has focused much of his attention to a program called, "Everyone Reads."

I contacted Judge Pratt and asked him for some of his personal insights of the Sixth Prescription, read a book-regularly:

> *God grants to each of us gifts and talents to serve the common good. We are presented in life with a series of adventures as we strive to discover and apply our talents. Reading gives us the ability to discern our individual talents and hone our skills as we make career choices. Most importantly, reading helps us replenish our soul and spirit.*
>
> *I cannot imagine my childhood without being frightened by the writings of Edgar Allen Poe, thrilled by the high seas adventures of* Treasure Island, *and socially challenged by* Fahrenheit 451 *and Orwell's* 1984. *Today I often find myself starting several books at one time.*
>
> *In each stage of my life, reading has been my silent partner. This partner has given context and expression to the miracles that surround me. This partner grants me access to a world in which the clamors of the market-place are barred. This partner allows me to control the unfolding story according to the dictates of my imagination. This partner empowers. This partner opens up to me a relationship with the Creator.*

Perhaps now you can better understand why, as I thought about the values behind the Sixth Prescription, I chose the quote, "Good things come in small packages." As Judge Pratt discussed in his life's journey with his silent partner, reading allows him to truly enjoy the "Good Life."

During the cold wintry months of Indiana, my wife Rhonda and I have the opportunity to get away from the pressures of our busy lives at home. We enjoy the warmth and substance of Florida, and try to relax and refocus on each other-two luxuries our schedules do not afford at home. One of the great pleasures and opportunities is to meet new and different people during our journeys away from home. One such opportunity came recently when we were privileged to meet Dr. Gene Landrum, PhD.

Dr. Landrum is a full-time professor at International College in Naples, Florida where he teaches courses on Management, Strategy, Entrepreneurship, and Leadership. His doctoral studies were on the "Innovative Personality" that has led to nine books on the nuances of success. Dr. Landrum is not only an educator and writer, but has a business background as a highly successful start-up executive who developed the "Chuck E. Cheese" concept of family entertainment, among other entrepreneurial ventures. Shortly after our introduction, I shared my passion for the "Twenty Prescriptions for Living the Good Life" with Gene, and asked for his input on the value of "Read a book—regularly." I am honored to include his insightful response below:

Books:
Life's Prescriptions for Success

I didn't read books, I read the library.
—Inventor, Thomas Edison

We learn more from books than we ever learn from the "tube" or partying. Travel and read and your adventures will be real and fantasy, but never dull, and you will be learning all the time you are experiencing. New words, new vistas, and new adventures are learned without you knowing that you are learning. The meanderings through the books allow you to go where others can't; the price is cheap, and the trip is fast. Never forget that Dorothy's journey down the Yellow Brick Road was not about finding a map, or a brain, or hearts, or courage. The metaphor was hidden in the action and the words. It was about hope. And that was what she really found in the Emerald City. The Wizard wasn't a con man at all. He was dispensing truth hidden behind life's debacles.

Books are one of the easiest means of escape into such a fantasyland where Shangre La is just a page away. Travel is easy and cheap. Later I will tell you a story about a boy who never left his mountain shack, but traveled throughout the world extensively through the power of books. When tested, this kid who never had parents, or even a pair of shoes, knew more Greek Classics than Greek scholars. When asked how he knew so much about Europe and the Middle East he said, "I visited them daily through books"

Reading is the conduit to the land of big and important words. Vocabulary is a by-product of our experiencing many words in different settings. Books are an exciting escape for the lonely; a way to find answers for those trying to create, and entertainment for those looking for excitement or fun.

The richest man in the world, Bill Gates, once confided to the media, "My favorite hobby is reading." The great emancipator, Frederick Douglas wrote that he owed all of his achievements to books. He wrote, "Reading and books were my pathway from slavery to freedom." America's master of historical fiction, James Michener said, " By the time I was twelve years old I had read forty volumes of Balzac." Former NBA superstar, Michael Jordan told journalists, "I read nonfiction so I can learn," Madonna admits to taking books to most of her concerts when she was getting started. She says, "My father forced me to read so I wouldn't watch TV. Now the "Material Girl" has settled down with two children and has written two children's books.

Oprah tells audiences, "I owe everything in my life to books." The star of television talk shows taught herself to read when she was just three years old. Within a few years she was reading to escape a horrid life in Milwaukee, and she has talked about hiding in a closet to read by flashlight so as not to be made fun of by her not-so-well-read stepsisters. It is not an accident that her sisters are still striving to survive while Oprah has become the first black billionaire in history.

Thomas Edison attended only three months of formal schooling. The inventor of the light bulb and holder of thousands of patents admitted to finding solace and information in books. He said, "I didn't read books, I read the library." The deaf inventor told of going to the Detroit library and starting out at A and reading every book until he came to Z. That is how he learned so much about the world of innovation. When Mark Twain set out for Gold Country in California, he had only one possession in his backpack. Yep! It was a dictionary. It was no accident that this self-taught man became the father of American literature and the author of *Tom Sawyer* and *Huckleberry Finn*. The famous author Danielle Steel grew up in boarding schools and was very unhappy. Her escape? Books! Steel writes, "I escaped into romance novels; I often walked into walls reading books." Ruth Simmons is now the President of an Ivy League College, Brown University. But Ruth didn't start out in life with much since she was the twelfth child of a poor sharecropper in the Deep South. Simmons says she owes her ascent to the top to the books she read on the way. She told the media, "I decided I would read every book ever written at the age of nine. I had a book in my hand all the time. People made fun of me." Her story is inspiring and shows how she allowed herself to compete with those kids with more money and privilege. "I discovered I could do everything these very wealthy, very well-prepared white women could do."

Creativity and long life have been attributed to reading. Books and reading makes the mind work and when it is working it is growing. When it is dormant it is dying. The Associated Press reported in March 2001, "Adults have hobbies that exercise their brains like reading are 2.5 times less likely to have Alzheimer's disease." In 2002 Harvard researcher Marilyn Albert reported:

> *Those above average in brain-derived nerve growth tended to be people who had made a lifelong habit of reading, attending cultural events and being physically active.*

Memorable Characters from Books

On the trek through life, we often forget people's names and other things, but we seldom forget memorable heroes or heroines from our favorite books. Who can forget Jay Gatsby, Nancy Drew, Tarzan, Sherlock Holmes, or Holly Golightly? Even the heroes from early comic books or plays like Peter Pan or Batman hold a strong place in our memory banks. An example is Batman. You may not remember a long forgotten cousin's name but you still remember Batman's sidekick, I'll bet. Robin was imprinted on those inner tapes that make you special from other animals. And many other things are also imprinted there and you don't even know it. So give yourself a chance and read about stuff you hardly care about and the knowledge build up will shock you.

We have all been conditioned by the #1 box office hero of all time, James Bond. The Bond heroics and mystique are mesmerizing. We don't even have to think about answering a question about his favorite line from "Goldfinger"–"The name is Bond, James Bond." Agent 007 first appeared in Fleming's "Casino Royale" in 1953 and is still a strong draw at both the box office for those who love his macho heroics.

Girls named Tara are never able to forget their namesake from Margaret Mitchell's classic *Gone with the Wind.* Shaw's Eliza Dolittle and Professor Higgins are quoted virtually every time one mate tries to change another in a reenactment of the Greek god Pygmalion, who asked the gods to make his statue come to life. Howard Roark and John Galt are now names taught in philosophy classes everywhere in America since they are the ones quoted from Rand's objectivism philosophy in her classics *The Fountainhead* and *Atlas Shrugged.* The renegade killer Raskolnikov from Dostevsly's *Crime and Punishment*—arguably the word's greatest psychological novel—is indelibly imprinted on our minds. And who hasn't heard an analogy on Willy Loman who is the classic looser from Arthur Miller's classic *Death of a Salesman.*

Books as Mythical Mentors

Thomas Carlyle wrote extensively on the Great Man Theory—concluding that the study of great men was the coup de grace of learning. "History," he wrote, "is the essence of innumerable biographies. Worship of a hero is the test of human nobility." Ralph Waldo Emerson came to the same conclusion, writing, "There is no history, only biography."

Joseph Campbell wrote extensively on the power of myths to guide our lives. He said, "A myth is a metaphor that makes heroes out of those who heed them." Campbell was right in the sense that it is often heroes from books that guide us and allow us to remove those self-imposed limits in our hearts and heads that say, "No you can't," or "That is way out of your reach." We adapt to the imagery of a hero, and without knowing it we emulate or imitate the way the hero would act. Protagonists out of books become fantasy heroes in our minds and end up altering the way we think and behave. Campbell's belief that myths make us more than what we could otherwise be, especially from heroes out of books, can be seen by his words:

> *Each of us is a mythical representation of our inner truths. Our job and other mundane experiences are merely symbols of a larger mythological meaning.*

An example of this can be seen in the way two great men behaved. Alexander the Great and Henry Schliemann conquered different worlds by identifying with great heroes from inspirational books, and they too, became heroes to a later generation. Alexander was so inspired by his hero Achilles from Homer's *The Iliad*, he carried the book with him into every battle, emulating Achilles prior to every engagement. The mythical modeling helped him conquer the world by the time he was thirty-five. The same book was instrumental in inspiring a poor German youth named Henry Schliemann. Once he had made his fortune he decided to travel to Eastern Turkey in search of the lost city of Troy. The stories of Helen and the fabled city of Troy had so mesmerized him in *The Iliad*, he decided to find the cities even though archeologists said it was only a myth. For Henry the city of Troy was real, and he dug until he uncovered the lost city, and it made him rich and famous beyond his wildest dreams.

No one who reads a lot writes poorly. Virtually every great writer in history was a voracious reader. When you read, you learn to write even when you are not trying to. While reading we are learning unconsciously. We learn new words, new sentence structure, proper syntax, and about interaction imagery and philosophy of life. All reading is good. Even comic books, since reading kids are not on the street looking for something to do or getting into trouble. But what has been found is that books can become mythical mentors. It is no accident that Shaq O'Neill, the great NBA basketball player plays the game like Superman, since he has the "Man of Steel" tattooed on his arm, printed on his car license plate, and on the rugs in his home. Michael Jackson was so inspired by his hero Peter Pan that he named his California ranch Neverland.

Carl Jung, the Swiss psychotherapist said it best, "It is not Goethe who creates Faust, it is Faust who creates Goethe." What Jung was implying was that the great German epic poet Goethe was influenced more by the imaginative protagonist he had created than the protagonist was influenced by his creator. Joseph Campbell said that, "Myths are imprinted Archetypes." He wrote extensively on this subject saying:

> *Each individual must find the myth that is fundamental to his internalized needs. Only a myth can help one live a systemic life with meaning.*

The quintessential example of escaping into books was author Frank I. Beam, an invalid child incapable of playing with other children. He was afflicted with a life-threatening heart ailment and bedridden, and escaped into the imaginative world of make-believe. He made up places that didn't exist to make life more palatable, not unlike Walt Disney some years later. Fairy tales permitted the youngster to cope. His imagination would lead to fourteen books on the great Wizard of Oz, who could fulfill the dreams of children despite the interference of witches, goblins, and meddling dwarfs. Beam wrote *The Wizard of Oz* in 1900. It was concocted out of the depths of his imaginative world of childhood, but as an adult it gave him a reason to exist and ultimately led to fame and fortune.

Books, Life and Learning—the Tragic Story of Bob Allen

There's a man who now teaches English Literature at Vanderbilt University whose story reads like that of pure legend. For Allen, books made life bearable and allowed him to travel while ensconced in a mountain cabin.

Bob Allen was born in the mountains of Tennessee to a very poor and illiterate family. His father and mother abandoned him as a baby, leaving him to be reared by an illiterate aunt and uncle. His Aunt Bevie Jones taught young Bob to read enough to read her passages from the King James Bible.

Allen's uncle was from the old school. When school officials showed up to take Bob off to the first grade, his uncle appeared at the door with a shotgun and said, "This kid will never see the inside of a school!" He lived up to his promise and Bob never spent one day in school. But he did spend his afternoons and nights reading from the Bible for his aunt who was losing her eyesight. After some time, Bob became bored reading the same stories and asked his aunt if he could go into town to find some other books to read. Like Thomas Edison before him, Bob went to the library and started at A and read the whole library to Z. Bob became enthralled, strange as it may seem, with English authors, especially William Shakespeare, and read and reread all his works.

Bob told reporters later, "I read 2000 volumes including *The History of Civilization* by Will Durant." Books became Bob's playmates and travel companions. "I studied literature in the context of history," he wrote, "from the earliest times to the present. Books were my pastime and playmates." During years of loneliness in the mountains the kid who never attended school became conversant and friendly with

Keats, Shelly and Byron. He learned Homer, Burns and Whitman, and then taught himself to read and write both French and Greek.

By the time Bob was in his late 20's, his aunt and uncle had passed away, leaving him alone and without a means of earning a living. Bob trekked down to the county offices and asked for a job. When the officials found he had never attended school, they said it would be very difficult to test him for skills. They were shocked at his scores and gave him a GED test, which he passed with higher scores than anyone in history. They then sent Bob to the local Junior College for further testing and discovered that the kid who had never attended school was so well read he knew more than the teachers.

Bob didn't own any shoes or suitable clothes, and was missing all of his front teeth. The poor but learned mountain kid had never ridden on an elevator. The county officials arranged for a scholarship and Bob graduated with honors. This earned him another scholarship to attend prestigious Vanderbilt University where he majored in English Literature. Finally in 1991 at age 42, Bob Allen graduated from Vanderbilt with a Ph.D. in English Literature. The boy who had never attended school was now a full-time professor despite having never attended primary, junior high, or high school. As a graduation gift, the school bought his first suit. Books made him more than he could have been had he gone to regular school.

Why People Buy Books

The majority of books sold are fiction. The most learned people tend to prefer non-fiction, but whatever the book, it is better than no book. In a survey in what women prefer to do in the bedroom, books came in # 1. More than anything, people buy books to escape (romance and mysteries), learn (non-fiction, biography, and philosophy), be entertained (fiction and poetry), as gifts (children's, cookbook's, and technical) or to get pumped up (self-help).

Many people read to improve, and the creative are often enthralled to find they are like the great people found in biographies. A New Jersey sculptor once wrote me and said, "Thanks for making me feel normal. My family taunted me for years about being abnormal and now I find I am like your great people—Edison, Bill Lear and Picasso." Validation for what makes us tick, drives us, or gets us excited can be found in books about great and creative geniuses. A fan,

John Eigerauer, a Ph.D., from Microsoft, read one of my books and wrote back about what it did for him.

> *I can't tell you how much your book* Eight Keys to Greatness *meant to me. You probably don't intend it to be psychologically liberating but it certainly was. I have never felt so liberated, so explained, so perfectly normal in my abnormality. While the book deserves accolades purely for its scholarship, and for its inspirational capacity, I want to thank you for the way it made me feel. Thank You for your time, your research, your prosaic skill, your keen observation, and above all, for understanding the subject you wrote about.*

Greatness-Often Hidden in the Heroes and Their Messages

It was no accident that the top five novels of the 20th Century were all exciting fictional treatises about how great life might be if one allows themselves to stroll outside the bounds of conversational wisdom. James Joyce's *Ulysses* was # 1; #2 was Fitzgerald's *The Great Gatsby;* #3 was a *Portrait of the Artist,* also by Joyce; #4 was a trip into erotica by Vladimir Nabokov with *Lolita*; and # 5 was *Brave New World* by Aldous Huxley.

It is interesting that the top five non-fiction books of the 20th Century also depicted people who were special. *The Education of Henry Adams* by Henry Adams was #1, followed by #2, *Up From Slavery* by Booker T. Washington. #4 was the autobiographical *A Room of One's Own* by Virginia Woolf; and #5 *Silent Spring* by Rachel Carson. Considered to be the best psychological novel was Dostoevsky's *Crime and Punishment.* The best philosophical novel was Rand's *Atlas Shrugged.* These works are often subtle to the point of burying the message within the actions and words.

Metaphors are easily lost in the message. True meanings are often hidden beneath the surface of the dialogue. The philosophical epic novel *Atlas Shrugged* by Ayn Rand was not about railroads. It was about the insidious destructive nature of communism for the human spirit. Until we remove ourselves from the details, it is difficult to see the whole. Don't confuse the map with the message or the metaphor with the words. What people say has little to do with what they really mean.

When Howard Roark in the classic novel *The Fountainhead* blew up a building, the message was about not allowing bureaucrats to steal his individuality and creativity. For Roark it was best to destroy his creation rather than have some self-serving bureaucrats destroy it or defile it. Protagonist Roark's words to the judge were the author's way of espousing her objectivism philosophy. When Roark said, "The world is perishing from an orgy of self-sacrifice. The creator originates. The parasite borrows and mutilates. It is a world in which I cannot live." Rand was telling the world to watch out or you will be made a slave to those who wish to control you.

Books–Fuel for the Soul and Antidotes for Anxiety

Stress therapists have long suggested reading as therapy for those unable to cope with life's miseries. While reading, it is difficult to get upset over outside forces and we often become so enraptured by the stories that life becomes far easier to deal with.

For a long time now we have known that positive begets positive and negative begets negative. We often become an external manifestation of how we think and feel with books opening many doors into fantasyland. The energy we can get from books and heroes may far exceed the temporary highs from ecstasy or other uppers without the insidious side effects.

We become as we think and it is the author's belief that we become as we read. Those who don't read will always find it very difficult to compete effectively with those who do read. Want it to be good and competitive? Read about great heroes and you will be able to mimic their deeds and action. Modeling behavior has been found to be more effective than just implementing behavior. After enough time, the escape into the Emerald City of the mind can make one far more than they would otherwise be.

Read three books in the next three months and I can almost guarantee you that you will have a larger vocabulary, no matter the books read. When reading we internalize the words. After much internalizing we become more like what we read which psychotherapists describe as conditioning. It won't be long before you will be speaking better, writing better and communicating better. After more time you will find yourself being labeled "well read," or "self-bred." Why? Because books and smarts are inextricably intertwined in nature and man.

Readers are fueled for a better future by books that can be antidotes for anxiety, and catalysts for creativity. Life is way too short to grow up not knowing and books can show us how to know. We seldom try to change things we do not understand. That makes knowledge the key to dealing with a fast changing world. Go find books that teach and titillate. They will change you and that will allow you to deal with the change and maybe even change your environment.

I implore everyone to read. And then to outline what you read for future reference. At a minimum, make notes on what you saw in the message or moral of what you read. Here are a few tips that I use when reading a new book.

—What did I find amusing or funny in this book?
—What was the meaning of the message hidden behind the words?
—What new word did I learn that I can use in my daily life or work?
—Can I be like the protagonist or hero?

If you would like more information on Dr. Gene Landrum, Ph.D., you can e-mail him at genelandrum@earthlink.net.

The Sixth Prescription is a "small package," but I hope this chapter will show you all the "good things" awaiting you when you "Read a book—Regularly."

When it comes to genius, Gene Landrum wrote the book.
—Naples Daily News, May 5, 1996

℞ Seven

BE TOLERANT OF OTHERS BELIEFS.

If we cannot end our differences; at least we can help make the world safe for diversity.
—John F. Kennedy

It is a good thing to demand liberty for ourselves and for those who agree with us, but it is a better thing and a rarer thing to give liberty to others who do not agree with us.
—Franklin D. Roosevelt

To know one's self is wisdom, but to know one's neighbor is genius.
— Anna Andrim

One of the greatest compliments our nation has been paid since its origin is the title "The Melting Pot." Truly our nation was founded on the principle and the hope that we would be a pluralistic society. As a boy, growing up in Germany during World War II, I knew how valuable freedom of religion was to every individual. Everyone watched as books on theology and religious icons were publicly burned and destroyed. Great thinkers like Dietrich Bonhoeffer, whose brilliant mind gave us classics in the field of religion like *The Cost of Discipleship* and so many others, became martyrs at the hands of religious intolerants in Nazi Germany. Such brutal injustice was the backdrop of my youth that cultivated a deeply personal desire to live and participate in a culture of religious tolerance.

I researched and wrote this book in the aftermath of the horrible tragedy of September 11, 2001. The memories of the Twin Towers, our nation's Pentagon in Washington, DC, and in the field in Pennsylvania will be etched in our minds for the rest of our lives. Once again our nation had found itself thrust into war. The face of terrorism is frightening and all citizens of this great country—no matter their political belief—believe in the importance of national security. It is not my intention to crossover into a discussion of politics or religion in writing this book. My passion is to set forth and support basic principles and values so that all may know a formula to "Live the Good Life." Nothing robs one more of this joy and privilege than intolerance. Intolerance is a thief that can sneak into the moral structure of our society and deplete one of its greatest riches-freedom. When we confuse unity with conformity we have been robbed of our pluralism, and intolerance will have stolen what has made us the great United States.

No better definition of "tolerating" exists than the one in *The American Heritage Dictionary, Second College Edition*, and I will give the direct quote:

> 1. The capacity for, or practice of recognizing and respecting the opinions, practice or behavior of others. 2a. Leeway for variation from a standard.
> b. The permissible deviation from a specific value of a structural dimension.

Let's explore the application of the Seventh Prescription. It simply states:

To improve human behavior, families and interpersonal relations leading to better lives and believing for more peaceful communities.

Improving human behavior by practicing tolerance begins in the home. I once heard that children are arrows in the hands of parents. There is no finer target we can aim our children toward than that of tolerance. Around our meal tables let us allow opinions of every family member to be expressed and respected. I know as the father of two sons and two daughters that some of my children's practices and behaviors were shocking at times; their choice in music and clothing were not those we, as parents, desired. The well-known psychologist and philosopher, William James said, "The art of being wise is the art of knowing what to overlook." Overlooking and demonstrating tolerance at home teaches our next generation how to improve their interpersonal relations.

The generations of the past in our nation did not always face these challenges with the capacity for tolerance. Religious intolerance is not a new blemish on the complexion of our society. We do not have to go back very far or search very deeply in our national history to find many embarrassing chapters. The Catholics have known much persecution and rejection and loss of privilege because of their beliefs. Catholic intolerance was witnessed as recently as the 1969 election of John F. Kennedy as our 35th President. Those of us who can remember and those who only know by reading history are aware of the obstacle of religious intolerance President Kennedy had to overcome in his race for the Presidency.

Another painful chapter in our nation's history took place June 27, 1894 in Carthage, Illinois. An angry mob of two-hundred people stormed a jail cell containing two brothers, Joseph and Hyrum Smith, Jr., the founders of present day Mormonism. Joseph and his band of followers were forced out of Pennsylvania, Ohio and Illinois because of religious intolerance. A nation founded on religious freedom was the ground on which these two men met brutal deaths as the price for their beliefs.

These examples are only a small portion of our nation's sometimes deplorable historical record on religious intolerance. The Jewish people have long known the brutality of religious bigotry. History and experience has led me to be passionate about the Seventh Prescription for "Living the Good Life." Our present generation will be challenged with maintaining its religious polarity, especially after 9-11.

In every community across our nation, we are recognizing a growing population of people who have more religious fervor than in past generations. Our fellow citizens who celebrate the Muslim faith are rapidly becoming a vital part of our culture today. Some of the finest teachers and professors in schools, many of the finest doctors I have met, and some of the most upstanding members of our communities are followers of the Prophet Mohammed, and call themselves Muslim—a religious title that can intimidate and threaten us, and arouse or awaken hatred. But what makes us great is the potential to embrace "structural dimensions," including religious differences.

Earlier I referred to the Kachmann Foundation Mission Statement. The statement closes with the words, "building more peaceful communities." Our hope is that not only Muslims, Jews, Catholics, B'hai's, Hindus, Buddhists, Hare Krishnas, Scientologists, Mormons, Jehovah's Witnesses and all those who are not mentioned (not by intention but by lack of knowledge for now), but those who hold no religious presence, will live peacefully in our nation's communities.

Toleration is defined as, "The official recognition of the rights of individuals and groups to hold dissenting opinions on religion.", *The American Heritage Dictionary, Second Edition.*

Let us all make together this declaration: *Be tolerant of others' beliefs!*

℞

Eight

EXPRESS HONOR, LOVE, AND RESPECT FOR YOUR FAMILY.

You know the only people who are always sure about the proper way to raise children? Those who've never had any.
—Bill Cosby, *Fatherhood*

I was the same kind of father as I was a harpist-I played by ear.
—Harpo Marx

If the statistics are true, by the time the average American youngster is six, he will spend more time watching television than he will spend talking to his father in his lifetime.
—Dr. James Dobson, *Children at Risk*

I found out the best way to give advice to your children is to find out what they want then advise them to do it
—Harry S. Truman

Hug.
—Annie Digeon, *Dad's Little Instruction Book (1995)*

Two terms that must be differentiated for the Eighth Prescription to be understood are "family" and "household." A family is different from a household. A household consists of all persons occupying a housing unit and includes family members and all other unrelated persons. On the other hand, a family is clinically defined by census reporting as, "a group of two or more persons related by birth or blood, marriage or adoption, and who resides together." I purposely took this definition from the U.S. Bureau of Census, *Current Population Report (Household and Family Characteristics)*, March 1982. Certainly much has changed in the definition of family since 1982. In the past 22 years, America's families have not only changed from traditional definitions, but are threatened by many adversaries intent on sabotaging honor, love and respect for family.

I know my introduction to the Eighth Prescription sounds more like a minister preaching from a pulpit than a doctor of medicine. However, in my practice, I have seen the important role family plays in a patient's recovery. The husband who is there with his wife when she must be told, "It is cancerous," offers a bastion of strength where the woman can seek courage and hope. The elderly patient finds comfort in the cold, sterile hospital room when surrounded by the warmth of children who love and care for them. Grandparents seem to have a special ray of hope when looking from their hospital bed, they can see scotch-taped to the room's walls, the grandchildren's hand-painted "Get Well" cards. Whomever the patient, any doctor or medical caregiver will testify, stands better odds of a speedy recovery when they have a family to support and anxiously wait for them at home. Because of this, I am a firm believer that "Living the Good Life" can certainly be attained by taking a good dose of "family." The definition of family, as I have experienced and witnessed goes far beyond the parameters of the Census Bureau's explanation.

A "family" is more than persons related by birth, blood, marriage, or adoption simply residing together. The great historical figure, General Douglas Mac Arthur, in his collection, *Reminiscences* (1964) said, "By profession I am a soldier and take great pride in that fact, but I am also provider, and infinitely prouder, to be a father. A soldier destroys in order to build, the father only builds, never destroys." Family is the place where unconditional love is given and received. Family is the source of security that prepares the child for all of life's threatening dangers. Family is where true laughter is enjoyed and unrestrained tears can be shed. Dreams are nourished in a family and failures are shared without condemnation and guilt. The family is where one treats others as they see themselves. A family member can make a point without making an enemy. Thoughts and ideas can be freely exchanged in a family setting.

I was especially impressed with the motivational book by Steven R. Covey, *The Seven Habits of Highly Effective Families.* Covey's "habits" are ones that would benefit any family relations. Let me give you a brief over view of these "Good Health Habits" that will build "Honor, Love and Respect" within any family that applies these principles:

Habit #1: "Be Proactive."

Covey challenges families to give gifts to each member that will enable them to exercise their freedom to choose. By cultivating self-awareness, conscience, imagination, and independence, family members will learn to "take a pause" between external stimuli, and their response, and properly use these gifts to make the best choices. I really appreciate Covey's suggested "fifth human gift" that enhances each of the other gifts; "A sense of humor."

Habit #2: "Begin with the End in Mind."

This habit simply stated is "To create a clear, compelling vision of what you and your family are all about." It was profound to read that, when a family has a clear destination in mind, it will affect every decision along the way. I know it was critically important in the establishment of the Kachmann Foundation to have a clear mission statement. Along with the board, I have continually gone back to the "mission statement" to clarify the direction and choices that have to be made. Why should we do less for our families? Covey states that creating a vision of what we want our families to be like, what we want to live and stand for requires asking members some tough questions. I would like to quote some of these questions. (Page 77):

"What kind of family do we really want to be?"
"What kind of home would you like to invite your friends to?"
"What embarrasses you about your family?"
"What makes you feel comfortable here?"
"What make you want to come home?"
"What makes you feel drawn to us as your parents so that you are open to our influence?"
"What makes you feel open to our influence?"
"What do we want to be remembered by?"

Covey challenges families to take time together to discuss and interact with each other about these critical questions in developing a "Family Mission Statement." On page 64, Covey gives a great example of a family mission statement that I would like to include in this chapter:

"Our family mission: To be always kind, respectful, and supportive of each other, to be honest and open with each other, to keep a spiritual feeling in the home, to love each other unconditionally, to be responsible, to live a happy, healthy, and fulfilling life, to make this home a place we want to come home to." Isn't that awesome?!

Habit #3: "Put First Things First."

Basically, Covey wants families to prioritize the family by establishing "Family Times" and one-on-one with each individual family member. Buy the book and read this habit! Turn the mission statement into the "family constitution."

Habit #4: "Think Win—Win."

Habit #5: "Seek First to Understand—Then to be Understood."

Habit #6: "Synergize."

These last three work together as "Root, Route, and Fruit." When all three of these come together successfully they produce what Covey calls, "The most phenomenal magic in family life. Mutual respect and understanding will always produce creative cooperation, and that is magic."

Habit #7: "Sharpen the Saw."

As the chapter points out, traditions can be a great means to renew family spirit.

These are my brief interpretations of these truly "effective habits for a healthy family." Again, I challenge each reader to get a copy of Covey's book. Developing these habits will help families survive turbulent times, stabilize the home and produce successful families who become healthy, significant participants in our world.

I know all of this sounds idealistic, but that has never been unrealistic. The challenge to have these qualities in a family reminds me of a story of a young man lost in New York who asks an older man, a musician for direction; "How do I get to Carnegie Hall?" To which the older man replies, "Practice, son, practice." The same can be said for families. We are not perfect institutions but we can keep "practicing." The comedian Paul Reiser wrote in his book *Couplehood* (1994), "I grew up thinking my parents knew everything. I'm sure they didn't, but at least they were smart enough to fake it. I don't even know how to do that yet." Now that is being authentic.

It is perhaps overstated, but television and "over-activity" are robbing families of the great opportunity to spend time together. I know the expression, "quality, not quantity" is a much-used principle, that is true, but let me take this a little further by illustration. If you were starving and sat down for dinner only to be served one small bite of *quality* fillet mignon with two small pieces of *fresh* lettuce with just a *dab* of your favorite salad dressing, accompanied by a half-bite of *delicious* potato casserole, and finished off with one fork of the *most wonderful unimaginable* dessert—would you feel satisfied?—or robbed? I think many of our families feel robbed in much the same way. If anyone knows the demands of a career, please understand, I am a compassionate ear. I also know that many families require both parents to work to pay bills. Many of my co-workers are single parents struggling to make ends meet. In the midst of all this pressure, let's ask ourselves a question, "Am I living the Good Life?" If the answer is "No," maybe we need a dose of the Eighth Prescription, "Express Honor, Love, and Respect for Your Family."

There may be those reading this book right now who cannot relate. You are like many of the patients I have treated over the years who were victimized by an alcoholic or drug-addicted parent or family member. Perhaps you were abused at the hand of an angry father or verbally demeaned by a mother. The words, "Honor, Love, and Respect" do not go together with family for you. Let me first say these words to you sincerely-I am sorry. I am sorry for your loss of your family and grieve for your loss; but I also want you to know that there is hope for you. First, you can recover, and we at the Kachmann Foundation stand ready to help you find the necessary resources that can help you, not only heal, but secondly, be equipped to be the best mate and parent for your family—overcoming your family-of-origin pain.

Rx Nine

MAKE A COMMITMENT TO CONTINUE EDUCATION THROUGHOUT YOUR LIFE.

To keep a lamp burning, we have to keep oil in it.
—Mother Teresa

Not to know is bad, but not to wish to know is worse.
—West African Proverb

An organization that I hold in high regard conducts "Lifelong Learning" workshops offered at no charge. In the workshops they teach how to access more than 10,000 courses and programs provided by various Indiana educational providers. Learning consultants are available to assist potential students. They offer programs to improve skills and answer questions about returning to college. I am particularly attracted to the program's name, "The Possibility Network...Your Connection to a Lifetime of Learning." (If you live in Indiana contact their web site at www.indianalearn.com).

What a great word "possibility" is. There are so many other words connected with the word possibility—conceive, think, desire, welcome, adventure, potential, future, and I particularly like this one: maybe! These words almost put a chill up my spine because they conjure up the word "excitement." I once heard, "An optimist sees opportunities in every difficulty, a pessimist sees difficulty in every opportunity."

Unfortunately, the word "possibility" is linked with words like failure, unsuccessful, embarrassment, rejection, frustration, loss, incompetent and dropouts. These words seem to have one common denominator—fear.

Fear keeps many of us from committing ourselves to continuing education throughout our lives. The word "possibility" is one I have to confront every day in my profession. It is "possible" for my patient to recover, work again, use a limb again, see again clearly, speak, walk...it is all "possible." My job is to continue to educate myself so I am best equipped with the latest procedures, medicines, equipment and tools so I can help my patient achieve their "possibilities."

Not only do I like the challenges of my medical work as it relates to "possibilities," but I have found it exciting in my personal life as well. Music has always been a passion for me. As a child I was privileged to play piano at Carnegie Hall. (How did I get there? Practice, practice, practice—my mother saw to it that I did!) Music continues to play a vital role in my life. I have enjoyed concerts in my own community, and have experienced performances in many great art centers around the world. (One of my greatest desires was to put the Twenty Prescriptions into lyrics and music as an anthem for our program. I am grateful and excited that this is now a reality. A CD of "The Call of Life" by Jeoffery Benward is included in this book.) Now back to my love for music and how it relates to "Make a commitment to continue education throughout your life."

At age 65, I wanted to return to my roots of playing the piano, something I had not done since my childhood. It had been so long ago that most of what I learned had, over the years, escaped me. But it was a "possibility." Not only did I want to relearn the piano; I have always enjoyed listening to the saxophone-another "possibility." Both of these pursuits required overcoming some fears, such as, "I am too old to learn anything new," " I don't have the time," "What if I have to play in a recital with a bunch of kids who play better than I do?" But I was still haunted by the word "possibility." I bought the keyboard and saxophone, contacted the necessary teachers and signed up for regular lessons. Along with my lessons, I rise early every morning before going to the office or surgery, and spend twenty minutes on the piano and twenty minutes on the saxophone practicing. "Possibility!" This past Christmas while dining with some friends and sharing my commitment to continuing self-education, I was coerced into performing a Christmas concert on the saxophone. There in the living room with my friends, I gave a rousing rendition of "Jingle Bells", and concluded with "We Wish You a Merry Christmas." It was great fun as my wife and friends joined in singing, and Christmas was very special. Now I am thinking that I love the song "Send In the Clowns," and there is a "possibility" that I can perform it on stage in concert with the "Voices of Unity Choir," a talented group of young people who have made a commitment to adopt the "Twenty Prescriptions" into their personal character development, and even perform by singing the Prescriptions in their inspirational concerts.

You, too, can achieve some great "possibilities" in your life. It is never too late! Make a commitment now to continue educating yourself throughout your life. Maybe it is to finish your high school education, or college education. Perhaps you would like to learn an instrument, take voice lessons, join a choir, learn to paint, or take a cooking class. There are many possibilities; all there is to do is: "Make a commitment to continue your education throughout your life." Take a regular dose of this Prescription and see if you don't "Live the Good Life."

Rx Ten

SHOW RESPECT FOR ALL LIFE, HUMAN AND ANIMALS.

He that respects not, is not respected.

—George Herbert

Constant kindness can accomplish much–as the sun makes ice melt, kindness causes misunderstanding, mistrust, and hostility to evaporate.

—Albert Einstein

Much has been said and is yet to be said in this book about the treatment of others in human relations. So far we have prescribed the following:

Rx #1 Treat others the way we want to be treated.
Rx #2 Be honest and do not steal from others.
Rx #3 Treat life with care-avoid risky behavior.
Rx #4 Show respect for authority figures in our lives.
Rx #5 Do not allow abuse of others to go unnoticed.
Rx #6 Read a book—regularly.
Rx #7 Be tolerant of others' beliefs.
Rx #8 Show love, honor and respect to our families.
Rx #9 Make education a lifetime process.

Adopting these values will build personal character and promote peace in our local and global community-certainly a hearty Prescription for "Living the Good Life." Prescription Ten reinforces six of the previous prescriptions by showing respect for human life, but now we add another dimension— animal life.

Children growing up in the 1960s were the first generation to be influenced by television, and so much of the programming related to animals and their relationships with humans. Remember Lassie protecting Timmy and his family, or "Rin Tin Tin" saving the Cavalry and looking after the Fort? One title of a show summed up the relationship between a young boy and his horse: "My Friend Flicka." Roy Rogers rode into danger and often into the sunset with "Trigger," while Dale Evans rode "Buttermilk." None, of that time, will ever forget the Lone Ranger's command, "Heigh-Ho, Silver! Away!" And speaking of horses, "A horse is a horse, is a horse, of course, unless the horse is a special horse," at which time the "Special Horse" would respond, "I am Mr. Ed." It was amazing—a talking horse. We were safe, not only by land, but also by sea because of a special friend, "Flipper," who guarded the oceans and his beloved friends.

Television wasn't the first to introduce us to the Animal Kingdom with affection. What child doesn't remember "Winnie the Pooh," and of course, "Tigger" too? Dorothy loved a "Lion" who was lacking in courage. All generations have enjoyed, and will continue to enjoy the animal world because of Mr. Disney's characters that we grew up with and continue to love in adulthood: Mickey and Minnie Mouse, Pluto, and Goofy. A whole new set of animals was introduced through animation in "The Jungle Book." And thankfully children are currently taught respect for the Animal Kingdom through movies like "Lion King," and the deep seas explored and appreciated in "Finding Nemo."

Children's hearts are strangely and uniquely attached (seemingly automatically) to the animal world. Special love exists with a child and their first pet. Whether it is that goldfish, turtle, gerbil, cat, dog, or pony—it will always be their first love. Most children's first memory of a funeral and penetrating questions of death stem from the loss of the family pet.

There is no more special love and emotional attachment than grandparents feel toward their grandchildren. I am blessed with seven beautiful grandchildren, all of whom bring great joy to my wife, Rhonda and me. In the writing of this chapter, I am reminded of my granddaughter Samantha's uninhibited adoration of all animal life. I have seen Samantha cuddle one of the most basic creatures on earth—a worm!

Rhonda, my wife, is "Aunt Rhonda" not only to her own special nieces and nephews, but also to an "extended family". One of these "adopted nieces" is a young lady named Maggie. My youngest child, Heidi, used to baby-sit for Maggie, who now attends Indiana University. Over the years we have maintained close relations with Maggie and her family. Maggie's special friend growing up was a black and white Lancier puppy. With Maggie's permission, her father allowed me to reproduce Maggie's letter to "Ariel," after her friend became afflicted with cancer, and had to be put down.

Ariel,

I remember the day you came into our lives. A little scared, but yet confident and majestic. You walked into greet your friend Pebbles and meet your new owners. Your fur was beautiful black and white colors—everyone's favorite cow. Then one day our hearts were filled with fear that we were going to lose you. You came home with three legs, but that didn't harm your pretty smile and puppy personality. Though we joked you kept going until another tragedy occurred and we tried to savor every moment possible with you. Now that you are gone, we are all weakened. Even though you're gone , you will always remain in our hearts with fond memories as our puppy, Ariel.

Maggie

I have often wondered what happens, when it takes place, that we lose that special bond with the Animal Kingdom. I derive much pleasure from the beautiful green and purple hummingbirds rapidly fluttering their wings around our cottage at the lake. Walking early in the morning and watching the lakeside turtles and seeing bluegills and bass just below the water's surface is an experience I love to share. I know not all have this kind of opportunity, but we are so fortunate to have parks and zoos; and a short drive will place us in the rural communities where animals can be observed. That, in turn, will bring a grounding and re-connection with the wonders of animal life that was once confined to our childhood.

Perhaps there is a new revived interest in man's relation to animals with movies like "Seabiscuit." This is a marvelous true story of how a nation, struggling through a Depression that seemed hopeless, was inspired by a man and a horse. "Seabiscuit" has shown respect of life, when the lack of such, could have cost him his life. He responded and rallied, and gave a nation a sense of destiny, despite incredible odds. Not only the horse, but also a man, was saved. Perhaps destiny brought them together to save each other and give us all an inspiring story.

Perhaps I sound sentimental, but I believe it goes deeper than simple emotions. We share this planet with many wonderful creatures, and it is my conviction that we should do all we can to preserve and protect, and show respect for all forms of life. I appreciate efforts across the country such as the "Second Chance Wildlife Rehabilitation Center" in my hometown, and other organizations that are doing all they can to show respect for animals. I close with a great quote from the Prophet Mohammed. Assuredly if we are "Living the Good Life" we should help all forms of life, including animals.

Whoever is kind to creatures of God is kind to himself.

—Mohammed

℞

Eleven

AVOID VIOLENCE, PRACTICE NON-VIOLENCE, SUPPORT PEACE.

Lord, make me an instrument of your peace;
Where there is hatred, let me love;
Where there is injury, pardon;
Where there is doubt, faith;
Where there is despair, hope;
Where there is darkness, light;
And where there is sadness, joy.
Grant that I may not so much seek
To be consoled as to console;
To be understood as to understand;
To be loved as to love.
For it is in giving
That we receive;
It is in pardoning
That we are pardoned;
And it is in dying
That we are born into eternal life.

—St. Francis of Assisi

Let every girl, let every woman, let every mother here (in Israel)-and there in my country (Egypt)–know we shall solve all our problems through negotiations around the table rather than starting a war.

—Anwar Sadat

It takes in reality only one to make a quarrel. It is useless for the sheep to pass resolutions in favor of vegetarianism while the wolf remains of a different opinion

—Dean William R. Inge

The air of an argument or discussion should not be victory but progress.

—Joseph Joubert

The fall of the year 2000 was an exciting time in my life. Because of the vision of the "Twenty Prescriptions for Living the Good Life." Early in the fall, I was invited to an inner city, cross-cultural church to present the Prescriptions to the congregation. It was quite a thrill to see the reception of the peo-ple as I shared these simple life-principles that could make a difference to our community if practiced. At the close of the presentation, I was deeply moved by the warm welcome of the congregation and their eagerness to participate in spreading the message of "The Good Life." As I stood chatting with various congregation members, I couldn't help noticing a well-dressed, handsome, young man making his way through the crowd. His steps were deliberate, and his face was deter-mined as he slowly approached me. The closer he came the more I was sure that I recognized him as a former patient—but he couldn't be!

The former patient I knew was a gang member from Fort Wayne's inner city. I am not sure of all the details leading up to his tragic incident; all I remember was being called into emergency surgery. Upon my arrival at the hospital, I found a young man whose life was in the balance, and whose only hope was surgery. He was another victim of a violent gunshot wound to the head. As I prepared for surgery, I remember thinking to myself, "If this boy survives, what a sad future he will have to live." His speech would be affected, eyesight impaired, walking and hand skills permanently altered and mental skills tragically affected. Only time would tell if he would return to any form of a normal life. After surgery and many family and friends' prayers, the young man came through. Each day brought more hope of recovery. Daily, I would come to his room and not only discuss his medical condition, but also his plans for the future.

How grateful I was that this young man had turned his back to a life of crime and violence. Through his traumatic ordeal he had decided to devote his efforts to become a minister. Several years had passed since he was released from my care and now here he was, slowly making his way toward me, dressed handsomely in a suit and carrying his Bible. We hugged, cried and laughed together as he struggled to share the news that he had followed through with his ministerial preparation, and was serving as an intern in a program in the church where I had just spoken. If only other stories could have the same ending, regretfully, they do not. Not a week goes by that I do not have to deal with a tragedy as a result of an act of violence.

The same fall of 2000, I was the keynote speaker for the first annual "March for a Crime-free City". Over 2,000 people from the greater Fort Wayne community marched through the streets of our city, making their declaration that crime and violence must stop. As I marched with the Mayor, city officials, Sheriff, Chief of Police, community leaders and residents of my hometown, my heart flooded with emotions. Walking past homes, I wondered if a member of that family had been a victim of violence—perhaps a father gone from home, serving time, or a mother suffering from abuse at the hands of a husband, or a son or daughter who had been beaten, stabbed, or shot.

The march concluded at a large city market parking lot where a great rally was conducted. Choirs and soloists sang beautifully, and city officials spoke eloquently, voicing our grave problems. My heart was stirred when I saw the wife of a well-respected, well-known, and beloved husband who had been robbed, shot, and killed. Knowing I was going to speak was quite an emotional experience, but my mind was strangely occupied with an encounter I had just before stepping onto the platform.

The Kachmann Foundation had been asked to contribute a visual illustration to dramatically impact the occasion. The "Twenty Prescriptions" were presented on two 10' high by 4' wide signs along with a huge artistic rendering of the sculpture I commissioned, that will be permanently displayed at our new Juvenile Criminal Justice Building. The most dramatic display we made available was a long wall listing the names of all the victims of crime in the city of Fort Wayne since 1998.

Row after row, name after name—it was very stirring to say the least, and many people studied the plaque, looking for familiar names.

Before the ceremony, I stood in silence as I watched family members approach the wall. Their eyes would systemically, respectfully go through each year until they would arrive at one special name...that of their loved one lost to violence. One woman particularly caught my attention as she stood by the wall. It was as though she was unaware of anyone else around her. She tenderly raised her hand to the golden plate with a male name engraved on it. It was as if it wasn't a cold nameplate at all as she slowly caressed the inscribed name. I couldn't help watching her and found myself speaking to her without prepared thoughts. "This must be someone you loved very much," I said softly. She spoke to me while staring with a gentle smile toward the wall. "He was my baby, only nine years old." Then she turned to me, as though returning from a far away place. She recognized me immediately and with some disconcertion shared that I wouldn't know her, but she had been at the church where I had spoken.

I asked her to tell me the story of how she had lost her son. My heart ached as she told me how her little boy had gone to the kitchen to fix some Kool-aid while she and her family watched television. A car stopped outside their home, unnoticed, as it was a regular occurrence in the neighborhood. This car, however, was different as young men burst into her home. Entering the kitchen with shotguns they ruthlessly shot down the little boy. They were gang members on a revenge mission and had gone to the wrong house. They shot the wrong, innocent little boy; a life cut short that would now only live as a name on a wall, and a memory in the hearts of a mother and those who loved him.

Seated on the platform, I now stared at the wall and looked out over the crowd and gazed at the homes. "Something must be done," I thought to myself. It is because of what I witness in my medical experience, and share one-on-one with grieving families that motivates me to want to make a difference. I could have quoted many statistics from various sources, and given many illustrations from generous others who offered to contribute information to this Prescription. My heart told me I should be transparent and speak from my own experience. These are only two of many similar, heart-wrenching stories that have impacted my life, and I trust will stir your heart.

There is one last experience I would like to share in closing on this Prescription. My love for playing tennis affords me the opportunity to meet many wonderful friends, and has opened many doors. One such privilege arrived when I played tennis with J. Webb Horton, the tennis coach of Florida Gulf Coast University of Fort Myers, Florida.

Because of our off-court relationship, we often discuss "The Twenty Prescriptions for Living the Good Life." Coach Horton thought it would be good for me, and an opportunity to advance these Prescriptions if I met some of the faculty and administration of the university. Recently, during Spring Break of 2004, there was a special ceremony conducted on campus entitled, "Circle of Hope: A Healing Memorial of September 11." I was deeply honored when asked to participate in this occasion calling for "Peaceful Tomorrows." Many cries were voiced for effective, non-violent responses to terrorism. My heart was moved as we joined together to read aloud the following prayer by Joan Chittister, OSB:

Prayer for Peace

Great God, who had told us
"Vengeance is mine,"
Save us from ourselves.
Save us from the vengeance in our hearts,
And the acid in our souls.
Save us from our desire to hurt, as we have been hurt,
To punish as we have been punished;
To terrorize as we have been terrorized.
Give us the strength it takes
To listen rather than to judge,
To trust rather than to fear,
To try and try again
To make peace even when peace eludes us.

We ask, O God, for the grace to be our best selves.
We ask for our vision
To be builders of the human community
Rather than its destroyers.
We ask for the humility as a people
To understand the fears and hopes of other peoples.
We ask for the love it takes
To bequeath to the children of the world to come
More than the failures of our own making.
We ask for the heart it takes
To care for all peoples

Of Afghanistan and Iraq, of Palestine and Israel
As well as ourselves.
Give us the depth of soul, O God,
To constrain our might,
To resist the temptation of power,
To refuse to attack the attackable,
To understand
That vengeance begets violence,
And to bring peace-not war-wherever we go.

For you, O God, have been merciful to us.
For you, O God, have been patient with us.
For you, O God, have been gracious to us.

And so may we be merciful
And patient
And gracious
And trusting
With these others whom you also love.

We ask through Jesus
The One without vengeance in His heart,
This we ask forever and ever. Amen.

You can learn more about Florida Gulf Coast University on their web site: www.floridagulfcoastuniversity.com.

℞

Twelve

CELEBRATE OUR DIFFERENCES: SEX, RACE, BACKGROUND, APPEARANCE, AND DISABILITIES.

God does not make clones. Each person is different, a tribute to God's creativity. If we are to love our neighbors as ourselves, we must accept people as they are and not demand they conform to our own image.

—Henry Fehren

We all have come on different ships, but we're in the same boat now.

—Martin Luther King, Jr.

Grant that we may not so much seek to be understood as to understand.

—St. Francis of Assisi

Who is wise? He that learns from everyone.

—Benjamin Franklin

The Twelfth Prescription begins with a word I hope grabs your attention: "Celebrate!" All other Prescriptions begin with words such as "Be," "Do," or "Make," but this prescription is meant to be different. The word "celebrate" means "to observe with respect, festivity, and rejoicing; to praise publicly with honor; to observe with appropriate festivities." As I am writing this particular chapter it is interesting to me that coincidentally, it is Martin Luther King, Jr. Day. Schools are closed in honor of this celebration and many "appropriate festivities" will respectfully focus on this great man's life and contributions. It is a tragedy he was so violently shot down in 1968. Who does not know the immortal words of his greatest speech?

> *I have a dream that one day on the hills of Georgia, the sons of former slave and sons of former slave owners will be able to sit down together at the table of brotherhood.*

As I look out my window on this Martin Luther King, Jr. Day, I too celebrate his life as I write this "Prescription for Living the Good Life." I am also reflecting that I was honored by the local chapter of the NAACP to receive the Martin Luther King, Jr. Award for the year 2001. Certainly, it would have been an honor to send Dr. King a copy of the "Twenty Prescriptions" and have his endorsement. Somehow I believe he knows that not only our program, but also thousands of other programs, and millions of lives "celebrate" his dreams today.

The dream of Dr. King is meant to go far beyond race and include gender, background, appearance and disabilities. I feel strongly that "longing for the ideal, while criticizing the real" is evidence of immaturity. On the other hand, settling for the "real" without striving for the "ideal," is complacency. I know that a "dream" sounds idealistic, but there are real things we can do, and that are being done, to improve our struggles with differences. Much has been done to improve the role of women in the workplace. Allowing maternity leave is a great stride taken by companies to celebrate the working woman's dual role of motherhood and professional career. But settling for what is real, and not striving for the ideal would only be indifference.

It would surely be idealistic to think that racial "profiling" would not be practical. Immaturity would be the attitude that criticizes the real present need for security during this time of international terrorism, but is it so idealistic to think of "celebrating" a neighbor who appears to be of Near Eastern background?

I have often witnessed the rejection of an individual whose appearance does not measure up to some expected criteria. It saddens me to see so many television programs devoted to the concept of "Makeovers."

Is it too idealistic to accept a person "as they are" rather than burst into applause when they return, after a makeover, looking like a totally different individual? Now don't get me wrong, I think we should do all we can with what we have to look the best we can within the framework of what we can afford or achieve. But let us not lose our ability to celebrate the uniqueness of every individual's appearance.

I paraphrase John Bradshaw, a leading Ph.D. and author on addictions by saying that addictions are any process people use to eliminate intolerable realities. Many patients and acquaintances of mine suffer because their backgrounds, or perceived standards of appearance, have become an "intolerable reality." As a result, their lives have become entangled in a web of addiction that is destroying them and inflicting great pain in their family relationships. Let's *celebrate*... we can be different!

When I see a disabled person, I do not see a mistake of nature, but rather a challenge to my character development. The way that I respond to that physically challenged individual determines the development of my character. I attempt to extend this example through how I live my life every day.

There have been great strides taken to make life more accessible to our physically challenged friends, and for that I am proud. But isn't it sad to think that after all these years, a disabled man, working in a public courthouse, has to file suit in Supreme Court to sue because he has been reduced to crawling up the stairs to get to his job? Let's not become complacent with the real accomplishments, but strive for the ideal. You can celebrate a disabled person's difference by offering a helping hand or even a friendly smile. The tendency is to be threatened by someone whose difference, because of a physical challenge, is intimidating, and we all feel awkward. I deal regularly with patients struggling with neurological diseases that affect their motor skills. Several of these patients have been some of the most intellectually stimulating people I have been honored to meet. Don't allow yourself to be intimidated—Celebrate!

I love living in an agricultural area of the country. Having grown up in New York City, one of the major contributing factors to my selection of Indiana University was the beautiful trees, and the desire to experience the rural environment. I am not a farm boy, but there are many things I've learned by celebrating the difference between a rural and an urban background. One thing I have learned is that if you ripen fruit too quickly, it loses its flavor. Tomatoes are often picked unripened so they will not bruise during shipping to the stores. Then, before they are sold, the green tomatoes are sprayed with CO2 gas so they turn red instantly. Gassed tomatoes are edible, but there is no match for the flavor of a vine-ripened tomato that is allowed to mature slowly.

Forgive my simple illustration, but I know we are not going to instantly change our attitudes toward differences—instant attempts at maturity will not have the ripened flavor of sincerity. But start slowly and deliberately to experience differences...maybe it will begin by going to an ethnic restaurant you've never tried...it might even become a celebration.

Reconciliation is more important than resolution. It is unrealistic to expect everyone to agree about everything. Reconciliation focuses on the relationship and makes resolutions that focus on the problem. When we focus on reconciliation, the problem loses significance and often becomes irrelevant. Because we are all humankind, we were intended to be reconciled as brothers and sisters in our diversities. Our unresolved differences have severed that relationship and we need to pursue reconciliation. We must use our resources, committing to reconciling our differences or our energy will be spent staying focused on our problems. Let's celebrate our differences and focus on relationships! Let's not emphasize what race we belong to, but be reconciled to the fact that we all belong to the human race.

It is my belief that fewer labels that distinguish "you" from "them" would make for stronger communities. I agree with author, Dr. Wayne Dyer that individuals "are not American, Californian, Italian, Jew, middle-aged, stocky, female, athletic, or any other label." We need to accept and promote citizenship of the world and bring an end to the labeling process. Let's look for what unites in every garden, every forest, every home, every creature, and in every person; and inner peace will be your reward.

Perhaps the clearest and deepest meaning of brotherhood is the ability to imagine yourself in the other person's position, and then treat that person as if you were him. This form of brotherhood takes a lot of imagination, a great deal of sympathy and a tremendous amount of understanding.

—Obert C. Tanner

℞

Thirteen

SEEK KNOWLEDGE, WISDOM, GOOD CHARACTER, AND PURSUE EXCELLENCE.

Do not believe what you have heard
Do not believe in tradition because it is handed down from generations.
Do not believe in anything that has been spoken many times.
Do not believe because the written statements come from some old sage.
Do not believe in conjecture.
Do not believe in authority or teachers or elders.
But after careful observation and analysis, when it agrees with reason,
and it will benefit one and all, then accept it and live by it.

—Buddha

Wisdom is knowing what to do next, skill is knowing how
to do it, and virtue is doing it.

—David Star Jordan

It takes wisdom to build a house and understanding to set it
on a firm foundation. It takes knowledge to furnish its
rooms with fine furniture and beautiful draperies.

—Proverbs 24:3 *(The Message)*

Character is destiny.

—Heracutus

Within the character of the citizen lies the welfare of the nation.
—Cicero

Some people get all As but flunk.
—Walker Percy

In his book *Character Matters*, Thomas Lickona cites on page 13 the 2002 report card on ethics of American youth. Lickona refers to the California-based Josephson Institute for Ethics that annually (since 1992) gives this report card from a national survey of thousands of high school students (over 12,000 in 2002). Here are some of the results:

— Three out of four students admitted to cheating on an exam in school during the past year.
— Nearly four out of ten said they had stolen something from a store during the past year.
— Nearly four in ten said they would "lie to get a good job."

I was stunned to discover that 80% of the students listed in the 2000 edition of *Who's Who Among American High School Students* admitted to cheating. Since this book began being published 20 years ago, this is the highest percentage—and these are America's brightest young people!

Encouragement is found on the horizon. Educators such as the 6th grade English teacher at Chicago's Willow Academy, Holly Salls, believes that education must include the teaching of virtues. In her new book *A New Vision of Character Education*, Ms. Salls outlines the character values she contends ought to be a vital part of any strong academic program. Here is a list of those character virtues:

— Responsibility for our work
— Thoroughness
— Organization and neatness
— Punctuality
— Self-control and willpower
— Honesty
— Working quietly out of respect for others
— Time management

—Being prepared
—Giving your best effort
—Concentration
—Perseverance
—Accepting disappointments
—Enduring things you don't want to do

Renowned psychiatrist Frank Pitman says, "The stability of our lives depends on our character—it is character, not passion, that keeps marriages together long enough to do their work of raising children into mature, responsible, productive citizens. In this imperfect world, it is character that enables people to survive, to endure, and to transcend their misfortunes." The core of all the "Twenty Prescriptions for Living the Good Life" is the necessity for character development and dedication to good health care habits. If we fail to transcend these values, individuals and our society as a whole will be set on a course of deterioration. Certainly we have precedence from our past. Historian Arnold Toynbee said, "Out of 21 notable civilizations, 19 perished, not by conquest from without, but by moral decay from within." It is my firm belief that if we, as a nation, were committed to the cause of character and health advancement as we are to the warfare against terrorism, we would sustain a meaningful peace in the world.

In my introduction, I referred to *Character Matters*, by Thomas Lickona. The "Ten Essential Virtues" that Lickona stresses are important for strong character development. I would like to distinctly list these as part of this chapter to accentuate their importance:

Wisdom
Justice
Self-control (also known as Temperance)
Love
Positive Attitude
Hard Work
Integrity
Gratitude
Humility

As Lickona points out, these ten essential virtues constitute what Aristotle referred to as the "Life of Right Conduct," (right conduct in relation to others and right conduct in relation to oneself).

One individual that I believe models the "Life of Right Conduct" is someone I would like to introduce to you now. He is Dr. Ben Carson, the Director of Pediatric Neurosurgery at John Hopkins Children's Center; a position he has held since 1984. Dr. Carson first received worldwide recognition in 1987 as the principal surgeon in a 22-hour separation of the Binder Siamese twins from Germany—the first time that twins connected at the back of the head had been separated with both infants surviving. Dr. Carson's story of growing up in poverty in Detroit and Boston caught my attention. He started out with terrible grades, anger, and low self-esteem. But once he made a decision to change his life by harnessing the power of his mind, nothing could stand in his way. Although I've never had the privilege of meeting Dr. Carson personally, I have read his powerful story in his book *Healing Hands* and have purchased vast quantities to hand out to children and young adults as a means of motivation. Dr. Carson wrote an article for the *Parade Magazine*, December 7, 2003, (pages 28-30) entitled, "Your Mind Can Map Your Destiny," and I feel that much of what he has to say explains the need for Prescription Thirteen:

> *Despite dire poverty, I had decided at age 8 that I wanted to be a doctor. In College, I majored in psychology and took courses that explored the psychological and functional aspects of the brain.*
>
> *At Medical school I decided to make neurosurgery my lifelong passion. I was impressed by the clinical presentation made by the neurosurgeons there, but the deciding factor was my own analysis of my God-given gifts. I had a tremendous amount of eye-hand coordination as well as the ability to think and visualize in three dimensions, a crucial skill. The brain does not contain many landmarks and a neurosurgeon must be able to imagine readily where all the numerous nuclei, tracts, and neurological pathways are situated.*
>
> *After the first glimpse around the dissection table, the landscape of the brain continued to hold a fascination for me. Two years later, I saw it again in a living patient. This time, as the dura folded back, the mysterious mass pulsated with life—and I had a sudden startling insight; this conglomerate of billions in interconnections was the actual physical thing that gave each of us our distinct personality, the intellectual and emotional characteristics that made each person unique.*

The organ system of the brain is one of incredible complexity and power. It can process millions of pieces of information per second. It remembers everything a person has ever seen or heard. For example, by placing special electrodes into parts of the brain that control memory, you can stimulate recall in an 85-year-old so specific that he could quote a newspaper article he read a half-century earlier.

One characteristic of the brain in particular makes us essentially human and distinguishes our brains from those of animals; the presence of very large frontal lobes. They enable us to engage in rational thought-processing, to extract information from the past and present, analyze it and use our conclusions to project a course of future action.

Animals are victims of circumstance. They can only react to their environment. But humans, thanks to our frontal lobes, can plan, strategize, and exercise control over our environments. We don't have to be victims who simply react.

I learned the truth about frontal lobes at age 10 when—not doing well in school and guided initially by my mother's firm hand—I made a decision to change my life's direction. Within a year and a half, by devouring book after book, I had migrated from the bottom of my fifth-grade class to the top of my seventh-grade class. This academic transformation was so dramatic that one might have suspected a brain transplant, if such a thing were possible. The actual change occurred in my self-perception and my expectations. I had gone from a victim to a master planner.

By age 14, my mind was plotting my future. Reading biographies of successful people, I realized that I could change my circumstances of poverty by programming my brain with the kind of information that would guarantee academic success. That, I believed, would allow me to choose my own destiny.

I encountered negative people who tried to discourage me and put a lid on my dreams. I chose to regard them as simply environmental hazards to be carefully swept aside.

My strongest supporter and inspiration throughout this metamorphosis was my mother. She was one of 24 children, had only a third grade education, and was married by age 13. She steadfastly encouraged my brother and me to read; though she never learned herself.

Many times, as I progressed from medical student to professor of neurological surgery, I was struck by the anatomical beauty of the brain and the extraordinary things medicine could do to improve the quality of life. Yet, at the same time, I became increasingly fascinated with the unbounded intellectual potential contained within that 1400-gram (3-pound) structure. The human brain, I came to realize, is simply a mechanical component of an entity of far greater beauty and power; the mind. I was awed by what an inspired and disciplined mind could accomplish.

Within every child's brain is a mind teeming with ideas and dreams and abilities unrealized. The greatest thing we can do-as parents, teachers, and friends is to nourish that potential, both intellectual and humanitarian, so that each can fulfill its promise to the benefit of mankind.

Dr. Ben Carson has said it better than I could, and I love the words he spoke, "Within every child's brain is a mind teeming with ideas and dreams."

Above the main door of every classroom building I suggest the following words be engraved:

"Be careful of your thoughts
For your thoughts become your words.
Be careful of your words
For they become your deeds.
Be careful of your deeds
For your deeds become your habits.
Be careful of your habits
For your habits become your character.
Be careful your character
For your character becomes your destiny."

℞

Fourteen

PRACTICE HEALTH—CONTROL: EXERCISE YOUR BODY AND MIND.

Commit yourself to a dream...nobody who tries to do something great, but fails is a total failure. Why? Because he can always rest assured that he has succeeded in life's most important battle ...he defeated the fear of trying.

—Robert Schuller

No farmer ever turned a field over in his mind.

—Gorge E. Woodbury

He that would eat the fruit must climb the tree.

—James Kelly

Let's talk sense to the American people, let's tell them the truth, that there are no gains without pains.

—Adlai E. Stevenson

There are no shortcuts to any place worth going.

—Beverly Sills

There is a word that leaves a bad taste in our mouths because it connotes grimness, and that word is "perseverance." The word is derived from the Latin prefix *per*, meaning "by" or "through; " and the root word *severus*, meaning "severe" or "strict." We persevere in this life through the strict practice of commitment, confidence, constancy, conviction, determination, devotion, diligence and endurance.

The verb "perseverate" is used in both psychiatry and neurology to describe a kind of pathology. Biologically, it refers to a particular brain defect that causes its victim to meaninglessly repeat themselves in speech or minor action. Psychologically, it is a reference to what Freud labeled "Repetition Compulsion"—the tendency to do the same "stupid things" over and over again despite the obvious outcome. (Now you know why I pursued neurosurgery instead of psychiatry-I tend to stretch psychological definitions-but you get the point!)

You live but once on this earth, why not let it be the most fulfilling, happy, enjoyable and successful life possible for you and your family? A lot of things that will determine your future are in your genetic structure. But your basic genetic structure can be influenced 90% of the time by your own actions.

There are many unfortunate illnesses that occur in humanity which are beyond our control. However, the majority of illnesses can be avoided by eating the proper diet, exercising your body and mind, and avoiding dangerous drugs, nicotine, alcohol, etc.

Obesity is rampant in our country, especially in the Midwest. Excessive weight causes a high rate of adult diabetes, hypertension, heart disease, peripheral vascular disease, strokes (cerebrovascular disease), lumbar degenerative disc disease, degenerative arthritis of the hips and knees. There are many other conditions, but these are the main ones.

Adult diabetes is mostly related to weight gain and can be totally avoided by maintaining a normal weight and exercising regularly. Dr. Leonard Mastbaum, Endocrinologist at Lutheran Hospital in Fort Wayne, Indiana has termed it "diabesity!" The complications of diabetes are frightening; blindness, stroke, cerebrovascular disease, coronary artery disease, renal failure, and neuropathy (paresis), just to name a few.

I would like to take the rest of this chapter and devote it to challenging the reader to "Practice health control" by exercising the body and mind. Exercise causes secretions of your own hormone (endorphins) which gives a feeling of exhilaration, clears your mind and gives you energy. It also reduces your weight, makes you look good and improves your self-image.

As we age, stiffness and spinal pain is a common complaint. By adopting a daily routine of stretching, especially after age 40, this can be avoided 90% of the time. Also, as you get older, you need less sleep; so do your exercising in the morning when the rest of the house is still sleeping.

If you are a parent with young children, get in the habit of putting them to bed by 8 or 9 o'clock. That gives you time for yourself—exercise, music, reading, etc. This will bring your life back into balance. It will also improve your health and set a good example for your family. It takes work and discipline, but you will feel much better about yourself.

A man who has had an impact upon my thinking through his lectures and writings is Dr. Wayne Dyer. In his book *Wisdom to the Ages* (pages 159-160) he gives four suggestions for our daily life:

- *Give thanks every day for this temple that houses your soul. Give verbal appreciation for your liver, your eyesight, your pancreas, every organ, every inch of your body. Simply say "Thank you God for this always changing, and always perfect place for me to observe from."*
- *Become more aware of how you choose to treat this miracle of a body. Talk to it as you give it exercise, good food, and generous amounts of fresh water. "I bless you, wondrous body of mine. By being more aware of what a perfect creation you are, I will avoid mistreating you."*
- *Observe the changes that take place in your body with joy rather than displeasure. Refuse to call any part of your body flawed. God does not deal in flawed material.*
- *A body that is cared for has a greater opportunity to advance the spiritual life. It is out of the spiritual invisible dimension that the material world is created. Purity of thought will help you to maintain a pure, healthy body. Remember, thoughts heal the body, not the other way around. This is why a welcoming attitude of awe and gratitude toward the body is such an important factor in the enhancement of your spiritual life.*

Bring music into your life, learn to play an instrument, listen to music, teach it to your children, sing. Music will develop unused parts of your brain and improve your memory, especially as you get older. Learning a new language also expands your brain, even in old age. The language is deposited in a different part of your brain than English, and could be a great benefit to you.

I love a quote from concert violinist, Lucia Micarelli. If you want to enjoy a beautiful CD, I encourage you to purchase "Music From a Farther Room." Here are some of Ms. Micarelli's thoughts on music:

> *If life is a journey and we are all wanderers, music leads my way; sharing my joy when I am overwhelmed by the beauty of small things, whispering words of comfort when I am afraid. Music has been my favorite diversion, my safe haven, and my unconditional friend.*

Certainly these words should inspire all of us to spend a little time taking in the beauty of music each day.

Over the years I have made a strong effort to take care of my body in spite of my busy schedule, and it has paid off, contributing to my "Living the Good Life." My days are very full . I get up at 5 a.m., and go to bed at midnight every day. I do yoga in the hallway outside the operating room while x-rays are being done on my patient during surgery—taking advantage of every second in my life. In the morning I practice music for an hour—saxophone and piano, and I take music lessons twice a week in the evening. I trade stocks on the Internet to make some money for my charitable work. It also stimulates my mind and constantly expands my knowledge.

Many years ago I fell in love with the game of tennis. I found it challenging and stimulating, an activity that surrounded me with opponents I enjoyed, and it was rewarding to play. (I was honored to be inducted into the Tennis Hall of Fame!) All of us can find some activity to make a part of our regular schedule. I even have a friend with disabilities who has succeeded in finding some special means of activity to provide physical exercise. Senior citizens can take this Prescription well—just go easy.

I am 68 years old and feel good every day. It takes discipline and a lot of work, but it is worth it, because I am " Living the Good Life." Personally I feel I have tapped into *the energy, the force, the spirit, God,* or whatever it might be, but believe me, whatever it is, it works!

Exercising your mind is something a lot of us forget. We all have issues to deal with in our lives as we get older, but I think a lot of it can be avoided by exercising the mind. Keep busy! Play cards, play games, play music, do charitable work, travel, develop a hobby—*don't retire!* My good friend and tennis opponent Gene Landrum from Naples Florida, an author and entrepreneur, gave a lecture to retired people, which I attended. He made the statement, "Retirement is the beginning of death." While there is some truth to that, it doesn't have to be. Some of the healthiest senior patients I see in my practice are doing something daily to keep themselves busy. One of them worked for General Electric for 35 years, and has worked for the past 17 years as a carry-out in a grocery store! He interacts with people on a daily basis, exercising his memory, and gets plenty of bodily exercise, carrying their groceries for them. He looks great in his early 80s.

Of course, any good thing can be taken into extremes. That is why I included the psychiatric term for persevering—"Repetition Compulsion," where physical good sense has been taken to extremes. Obsessive compulsions can be damaging in any area of life, not just drugs or alcohol. But that should not be an excuse either, for not exercising regularly.

So why don't we practice health-control and exercise our bodies and minds? How about the words: confidence, commitment, determination, constancy, and endurance-words all wrapped up in the word "Perseverance!"

I'd like to close this chapter with another quote from Dr. Wayne Dyer's book *Wisdom of the Ages*, page 165:

> *I suggest that you literally kick downstairs any and all attitudes that you may be cultivating, or that you have already adopted, which identifies yourself as aging, or a limited body. To get this process started, I suggest you:*
>
> — *Talk to your body and force it to become more active, despite its objections. If you have accustomed your body to living as a couch potato, it will resist walking and running and being dragged through exercise routines. Note these protests, then do it anyway.*
>
> — *Resist impulse to label yourself with descriptions that limit you in any way. Statements such as "I'm not good at..." or "I've never been interested in..." only serve to strengthen your self-image of limitation. You can be good at, and enjoy anything if you decide to.*
>
> — *Put yourself through a self-improvement project that is designed to maximize your state of mind, body, spirit, and soul. Write your own personal curriculum and apply it each day.*
>
> — *Take classes in something new or unfamiliar, such as archery, bridge, yoga, meditation, tai chi, tennis, dancing, or anything that you have never experienced before.*

℞

Fifteen

DO NOT ABUSE YOUR BODY-AVOID TOBACCO, ALCOHOL, AND DRUGS.

Temperance is the modeling of one's desires in obedience to reason.
—Cicero

Choose rather to punish your appetites than to be punished by them.
—Tyrus Maximus

Sobriety's a real turn-on for me. You can see what you're doing.
—Peter O'Toole

I've never been one who thought the Lord should make life easy; I've just asked him to make me strong.
—Eva Bowring

Intemperance is the Physician's Provider.
—Publius Syrus

In the last several Prescriptions I have shared openly and transparently from my own experiences, and hope it was meaningful in my presentation. The Fifteenth Prescription is the one I feel most passionately about, and so have deep convictions and feelings about this topic. As a physician I have witnessed the utter destruction these substances can have upon so many lives.

As a neurosurgeon, I constantly deal with the complications of smoking—lung cancer with metastatic spread to the brain and spine (90% of the time it leads to death within a few months), emphysema (stiff lungs), peripheral vascular disease, coronary and cerebrovascular disease, and premature aging are most common.

Smoking ages people. They appear 10-20 years older than they are. I pointed this out recently to a patient of mine in an attempt to get her to stop smoking. She started to cry. She said, "You know Doctor, my husband is 10 years younger than I, and my smoking makes me look 20 years older than him!"

Here are some statistics that I have gathered over the years of my practice:

- Almost 180,000 Americans die each year of cardiovascular disease caused by smoking.
- The risk of heart disease is 70 percent higher among smokers.
- Thirty-five percent of smoking-related deaths from heart disease occur before age 65.
- A smoker is two times more likely to die of a heart attack than is a nonsmoker, and the risk is even greater for heavier smokers.
- A smoker who has a heart attack and continues to smoke is six times more likely to have a second heart attack than is one who stops smoking.

I saw a number of patients last year, especially women in their 40's, who were dying from lung cancer with metastasis to the brain. One of these patients was a heavy smoker, and the second contracted the disease from secondary smoke.

This attractive blond lady came to me with horrible pain in her tailbone radiating down her leg. Usually this would be indicative of a disc problem, but after a thorough examination I found a tumor on the sacral area of the spine. Then the culprit walked into the room. Her husband had just entered after parking the car, and I picked up the odor of smoke. I immediately became suspicious–although the patient showed no signs of smoking, she might have lung cancer from secondary smoke, and we found that to be the case.

This beautiful lady died within six months. Her husband's health was so impaired from his habit that he could not walk down one flight of stairs so I could show him his wife's x-rays and give him the news of his wife's prognosis.

More than 50,000 Americans die each year of exposure to secondhand (passive) smoke. As a result, most states have enacted laws limiting smoking in public places.

Inhaling secondhand smoke causes your heart to beat faster, you blood pressure to increase and the level of carbon monoxide in your blood to rise. Side-stream smoke from a burning cigarette contains twice as much tar and nicotine as does inhaled smoke, three times more of a cancer-causing compound called 3,4-benzypyrene, five times more carbon monoxide and possibly 50 times more ammonia.

The deadly effects of secondhand smoke are far-reaching and clear:

- In the United States, 27 percent of homes with children age 6 and younger allow smoking, affecting 9 to 12 million children.
- Children exposed to secondhand smoke are at greater risk of developing asthma, ear infections, pneumonia and bronchitis.
- Infants and children regularly exposed to secondhand smoke are hospitalized 7,500 to 15,000 times each year for treat ment of respiratory tract infections.
- Approximately 3,000 nonsmokers die each year of lung cancer as a result of secondhand smoke.
- About 40,000 nonsmokers die each year as a result of cardio vascular disease as a result of secondhand smoke.

The social aspects of smoking are also horrendous. The odor is offensive to non-smokers, it contaminates a smoker's home, their car, and their clothing. Employers don't like to hire smokers, teenagers don't like to date smokers. Insurance is higher for smokers. The smoke residue in your home can lower the sale price of your home should you decide to sell it. There are many negative details to smoking. The trick is to never start in the first place. For once you have acquired the habit, it is a difficult one to break.

Most cigarette smokers start early in life. Among smokers born since 1935, more than 80 percent started smoking before age 21, and more than half started before age 18. Today, a million teenagers begin smoking each year. An increasing number of them are female.

I have had the opportunity to present the Twenty Prescriptions at various local schools, and was shocked at the number of high school students who admitted to smoking. The principal of one high school told me easily 95% of his students were smokers. I challenged the students in my presentation by saying I would make a pizza available to any student who would quit smoking for one day. Much to my disappointment, there were no takers.

Even though smoking has generally declined since the mid-1960s, an increasing number of teenagers smoke. This group continues to be a major target for advertising by the tobacco industry.

— More than one in four high school students smoke cigarettes.
— More than one in five high school students say they smoked a cigarette before age thirteen.
— Almost two-thirds of 11-17 year old students who smoke got their first cigarette from a friend.
— The younger people are when they start smoking, the more likely they are to become addicted to nicotine.
— A high percentage of teenagers who smoke are in families in which one or both parents smoke.

Students who stated they smoked at least one cigarette in the past 30 days:
— 12th graders—26.7%
— 10th graders—17.7%
— 8th graders—10.7%

How friends affect youth smoking:
— 44.1%—"Almost all my friends smoke."
— 12.4%—"Some of my friends smoke."
— 1.0%—"None of my friends smoke."

Education does not appear to be an effective deterrent to smoking among teenagers. Nine out of ten teenagers surveyed believed that smoking was harmful to their health. And 85 percent of those who smoked said that they didn't plan to be smoking for more than five years. Most of the teenagers who took up smoking had been adamantly against smoking in their younger years. Parents who continue to smoke with no visible ill effects can have a substantial influence. In such situations, teenagers' concerns about smoking diminish, and many take up smoking.

If you are parents and would like more information contact: www.philipmorrisusa.com or call toll free 1-800-768-7397 and ask for "Raising Kids Who Don't Smoke, Peer Pressure, and Smoking," If you live in or around Northeast Indiana call Smoke Free Allen County at 1-260-424-7881.

I have never tried illegal drugs, and I avoid addictive pain medication unless they are clearly indicated. In my practice I see addictive pain medications prescribed for reasons that I sometimes don't understand, and this is a problem, I feel, throughout our country. Do not accept a narcotic from your health care provider unless something serious is going on in your body. If you don't know what your condition is, I would try to avoid a narcotic unless the pain is unbearable, and all other avenues of pain relief have been explored. There are many alternatives that can aid in pain relief, analgesics, muscle relaxers, exercise, psychotherapy, and pain support groups to name a few. I have seen patients who have tension stress problems walking around taking narcotics. Their health care provider is misinterpreting the problems the patient is having. I probably see one to three patients a day in this condition, and that concerns me a great deal.

Chronic narcotic medications should only be prescribed for clear-cut pain conditions where one knows the cause. Health care providers frequently confuse chronic pain stress and this is a serious problem throughout our nation. One patient told me recently that there was a "pain center" on every corner in Los Angeles. I saw two patients from California just this past week with this type of problem where addictive pain medication should never have been prescribed in the first place. I had another patient tell me recently that if a certain health care provider in my community stopped prescribing medicine, the whole city would go into withdrawal! This concerns me greatly! I sent that physician a couple of books about tension stress syndrome in hopes of educating that individual. I don't mention these instances because I only see them occasionally, but because it is prevalent in my practice, and I am concerned, and the public needs to be alert to the situation and aware of the dangers.

Alcohol is a drug, and affects many of our internal organs. It is not well known, but every drink of alcohol destroys a certain number of brain cells. Certainly the MRIs I have seen in people who consume a large amount of alcohol show their brain is a great deal smaller than that of someone who does not drink. The patients I see who consume a great deal of alcohol tend to have subdural hematomas (blood clots on the brain), memory loss, unsteady gait, ataxia (the inability to coordinate muscular movements), and personality changes.

This brings to the forefront the question,"What is alcoholism?" *The Mayo Clinic Family Health Book (New Third Edition)* defines it as "a chronic, progressive and often fatal disease". The condition involves a preoccupation with alcohol and impaired control over its use. You may continue to abuse alcohol despite serious adverse health, personal, work-related and financial consequences. Alcoholism may involve a physical dependence on the drug alcohol. Genetic, psychological and social factors all contribute to the addiction."

Most alcoholics deny they have a problem. Other signs and symptoms of alcoholism include:

- Drinking alone or in secret.
- Forgetting conversations or commitments.
- Making a ritual of having drinks before, with or after dinner and becoming annoyed when the ritual is disturbed or questioned.
- Losing interest in activities and hobbies that used to bring pleasure.
- Irritability as usual drinking time nears, especially if alcohol isn't available.
- Keeping alcohol in unlikely places at home, at work or in the car.
- Gulping drinks, ordering doubles, becoming intoxicated intentionally to feel good or drinking to feel "normal."
- Having legal problems or problems with relationships, employment or finances.

Each of these may be continuous or periodic. It's the physical dependence (addiction) to alcohol—demonstrated by tolerance and withdrawal symptoms—and compulsive behavior related to its use that usually distinguishes alcoholics from problem drinkers.

Continued alcohol use over time can produce a physical dependence on alcohol. However, drinking by itself is just one of the risk factors that contributes to alcoholism. Other risk factors include:

- **Age.** People who begin drinking at an early age—in their teens or earlier—are at a higher risk of becoming alcoholics.

- **Genetics.** Your genetic makeup may cause imbalances in one or more of several brain chemicals and increase your risk of alcohol dependency.
- **Sex.** Men are more likely to become alcoholics than are women. But the incidence of alcoholism among women has increased in the past 30 years.
- **Family history.** The risk of alcoholism is higher to people who had a parent or parents who abused alcohol.
- **Emotional disorders.** Depression or anxiety places you at a greater risk of abusing alcohol to temporarily block out the turmoil.

Some disorders have manifestations that make a diagnosis easy. Alcoholism, however, often defies easy classification because its characteristics vary greatly from one problem drinker or alcoholic to the next.

To cope with this difficulty, Mayo Clinic has developed the Self-Administered Alcoholism Screening Test (SAAST). Based in part on the Michigan Alcoholism Screening Test, the SAAST consists of 37 questions. In use since 1972, the test can identify 95 percent of alcoholics ill enough to be hospitalized.

The test aims to identify behavior patterns, medical signs and symptoms and consequences of drinking in the alcoholic. Here's a sample of questions from the test:

1. Do you have a drink now and then?
2. Do you feel you're a normal drinker (that is, you drink no more then average)?
3. Have you ever awakened the morning after drinking the previous evening and found that you couldn't remember a part of the previous evening?
4. Do close relatives ever worry or complain about your drinking?
5. Can you stop drinking without a struggle after one or two drinks?
6. Do you ever feel guilty about your drinking?
7. Do friends or relatives think you're a normal drinker?
8. Are you always able to stop drinking when you want to?
9. Have you ever attended a meeting of Alcoholics

Anonymous (AA) because of your drinking?
10. Have you gotten into physical fights when drinking?

If your responses match four or more of these answers, you may be at risk of alcoholism: 1. yes 2. no 3. yes 4. yes 5. no 6. yes 7. no 8. no 9. yes 10.yes

The social aspects of alcohol abuse, as in smoking, are appalling and alarming. It not only affects the health of the person drinking, but affects the people around them. It destroys marriages, relationships, and careers. The effects are generational—scarring the children and grandchildren of the one who drinks.

- In 2002, an estimated 17,419 people died in alcohol-related traffic crashes—and average of one every 30 minutes. These deaths constitute 41% of 42,815 total traffic fatalities. (NHTSA, 2003)

- About three in ten Americans will be involved in an alcohol-related crash at sometime in their lives. (NHTSA, 2001)

- In 2001 more than half a million people were injured in crashes where police reported that alcohol was present—an average of one person injured every two minutes. (Blanc, Say, et, al 2002)

- The highest prevalence of both binge and heavy drinking in 2000 was for young adults ages 18-25, the peak rate occurring at age 21. (SAMHSA, 2000)

- Alcohol is closely linked to violence. About 40% of all crimes (violent and non-violent) are committed under the influence of alcohol. (Bureau of Justice Statistics, 1998)

- Alcohol is society's legal, oldest, and most popular drug. (Narcotic Foundation of America, 2002)

- Alcohol-related fatalities are caused primarily by the consumption of beer (80%), followed by liquor/wine at 20%. (Runge, 2002)

- Those drivers ages 21-24 years old were most likely to be intoxicated (BAC of 0.09g/dl or greater) in fatal crashes in 2002. 33% of drivers 21-24 years old involved in fatal crashes were intoxicated, followed by ages 25-34 (28%), and 35-44. (26%). (NHTSA, 2003)

- For fatal crashes occurring from midnight to 3:00 am 79% involved alcohol. (NHTSA, 2003)

- The rate of alcohol involvement in fatal crashes is more than 3 times as high at night as during the day (63% vs. 19%). For all crashes, the alcohol involvement rate is 5 times as high at night (15% to 3%). (NHTSA, 2003)

- Drunk driving is the nation's most frequently committed violent crime, killing someone every 30 minutes. (NHTSA, 2003)

- In 2000, motor vehicle crashes were the leading cause of death for people from 1-34 years old. (CDC, 2001)

For more direct information go online at: www.madd.org.

If, as a result of reading this chapter, you feel that you are suffering from a life-controlling problem , there is a program I strongly recommend. Alcoholics Anonymous has developed the Twelve Steps of Recovery, that have resulted in countless success stories around the world.

The Twelve Steps are at the heart of the program of personal recovery. They describe the experience of the founding members of AA.

1. We admitted we were powerless over alcohol—that our lives had become unmanageable.
2. We came to believe that a Power greater than ourselves could restore us to sanity.
3. We made a decision to turn our will and our lives over to the care of God as we understand Him.
4. We made a searching and fearless moral inventory of ourselves.

5. We admitted to God, to ourselves and to another human being the exact nature of our wrongs.
6. We were entirely ready to have God remove all these defects of character.
7. We humbly asked Him to remove our shortcomings.
8. We made a list of all persons we had harmed and became willing to make amends to them all.
9. We made direct amends to such people wherever possible, except when to do so would injure them or others.
10. We continued to take personal inventory and when we were wrong promptly admit it.
11. We sought through prayer and meditation to improve our conscious contact with God as we understood Him, praying only for knowledge of His will for us and the power to carry that out.
12. Having had a spiritual awakening as the result of these steps, we tried to carry this message to alcoholics and to practice these principles in all our affairs.

The wonderful thing about the Twelve Steps is that the word "alcohol" can be substituted with any addictive behavior with the same results being achieved. I believe the most important word in the Twelve Steps is the word "We." This simple word informs us that the program cannot be worked alone, but requires the encouragement and direction from others who understand the problem.

Today, there are many Twelve Step programs, covering the entire realm of life-controlling problems. By simply using your Telephone Directory, you can make contact with the appropriate program for your needs.

You have already read the statistics and the facts concerning the consequences of abusing your body. If any of the descriptions apply to you, please do not delay in making the most important telephone call of your life! Get help today!

℞ Sixteen

HELP THOSE WHO ARE SUFFERING OR IN NEED.

Love cannot remain by itself—it has no meaning. Love has to be put into action and that action is service.

—Mother Teresa

Being unwanted, unloved uncared for, forgotten by everybody, I think that is a much greater hunger, a much greater poverty than the person who has nothing to eat...we must find each other.

—Mother Teresa

If someone listens, or stretches out a hand, or whispers a kind word of encouragement, or attempts to understand a lonely person, extraordinary things tend to happen.

—Loretta Girzartis

True kindness presupposes the facility of imagining as one's own suffering and joys of others.

—Joseph Joubert

Throw out the lifeline, throw out the lifeline, someone is sinking today.

—Edward Smith Clifford

The greatest reward of my life has come as a result of this Prescription being my life mission. I don't believe anyone can enter the medical profession and remain in the field of service if you have any other driving force than a desire to "help those who are suffering or in need." There is no gratification like that of helping relieve the suffering of a fellow human being. There is a great book written by Tim Hansel entitled, *You Gotta' Keep Dancing*. Mr. Hansel shares his story of surviving a terrible fall while rock climbing, and as a result, sustained injuries that caused permanent chronic pain for which he has no relief. One of the great healing powers of his life has come through love, concern, and encouragement of others. I was particularly impressed by one of Mr. Hansel's quotes:

Pain is inevitable, misery is optional.

Unquestionably, a common denominator for all humankind is that of suffering. Everyone I know in life has fear of some form of pain, whether it is physical, emotional, financial, spiritual, or grief from loss. All of us are called upon to endure an element of suffering during our life's journey. Despite the pain, we can choose not to be miserable, and learn to show genuine compassion for others who are suffering.

I believe the torment of suffering is when we ask, "Why?" and we don't seem to find any reasonable explanation. The misery accompanying the pain is particularly unbearable when another thinks they have all the answers. Sometimes it's the most tender expression of compassion not to offer an answer, but just lend a listening ear. Years ago there was a great commercial for milk featuring the Country Western singer Kenny Rogers. He was walking in a beautiful grassy field with an inquisitive little boy. As they strolled along, the little fellow looked up at Kenny Rogers and asked, "Why is the sky blue?" Kenny Rogers pondered for a moment, then responded, "I don't know." A little further on their excursion the boy asked, "Why is the grass green?" and again Rogers delivered a puzzled answer, "I don't know." Finally the child asked, "Do all my questions bother you?" And Kenny Rogers said, "No, how else are you going to learn?" Sometimes we learn more about life when we don't have all the answers.

I am not much of a traditional church-goer, and I certainly do not claim to have a total understanding of the Scriptures. However, I have appreciated the story of two sisters, Mary and Martha, I believe were their names. Their brother Lazarus died and was buried. In the midst of their suffering and loss they sent word to Jesus. Upon arriving, Jesus knelt by the tomb where his friend was buried and did one of the kindest acts, he wept. Sometimes we can take away the misery of pain and grief by simply making ourselves vulnerable and real with the afflicted.

When I decided to complete these Prescriptions, I wrote to many dedicated people to ask for their input. I have already shared thoughts from people like Sheriff Archey and Judge Pratt. When I wanted some insights on helping people who are suffering or in need, I wrote to someone outside the medical field. I contacted Rev. Dave Humphries, Director of Fort Wayne Rescue Mission. For years this ministry has been a vital outreach to the indigent and homeless—hurting people who come to our city and need help. A clean environment and three square meals are offered along with a message of hope for the downcast. I found Rev. Humphries comments especially poignant and would like to share then with you:

> *Helping those who are suffering or in need has been a dominant influence in my life. I believe all Christians are called to this, (as in Matthew's Gospel, Chapter 25, for example), regardless of their vocation, Christians are to gain their life through freely giving it, always by serving the suffering and needy. I have been much more richly blessed by my service than they have been as recipients. My ministry takes my focus off me and my needs, and places it on the needs of others. When I do that, I feel I am truly loving people in a non-self-centered way—which my faith calls me to do. So, to give your life away for the needy is to find who God created you to be.*

I salute you, Rev. Humphries, and all those who serve with you. What a life example you are, and what a positive force you are in our community!

There seems to be a growing trend what warms my heart and gives me hope. I watched on NBC's "Today Show" as they interviewed several adults and young people taking different types of vacations. Rather than taking a cruise or going to the islands—instead of enjoying a ski resort, or saving for that European trip, they were taking a non-traditional form of "vacation." Each were going to some remote part of the world, at their own expense, and doing something to reduce the suffering of that area's people. One young lady had taken her vacation to go to a South American area where the men were imprisoned. The children were undereducated and in desperate need of medical attention. This young lady was going to help teach these unwanted, uncared for children who were suffering or in need. I hope alternative "vacations" will be an increasing trend in our young society.

I am going to close this chapter with a story of a young doctor from my home town. I believe Dr. Jane Weaver is a beautiful example of "helping those who are suffering and in need."

Dr. Jane Weaver is a native of Fort Wayne, Indiana. She received her medical degree from Indiana University School of Medicine, then completed a five-year residency in general surgery at the University of Louisville under the direction of Dr. Hiram C. Polk.

Raised in a Christian home, Dr. Weaver felt drawn to missionary service as a teenager. This feeling only intensified as the years passed. She knew that some kind of missionary service would be a part of her life, regardless the direction her career as a general surgeon would take. During her residency, Dr. Weaver began investigating arenas where she could go as a missionary surgeon on a short-term basis. She had accepted a two-year contract with Indiana Surgical Specialists in Fort Wayne, but wanted to spend some time in missionary service before starting her surgical practice.

After investigating many alternatives, Dr. Weaver decided to go to Ecuador, and spent several months in a missionary hospital in Shell as a general surgeon. Shell is a small town originally built by the oil company of the same name, and is located where the Andes Mountains meet the Amazon jungle. The hospital there is operated by the HCJB World Radio as one of their many medical outreaches.

During her time in Shell, Dr. Weaver fell in love with Ecuador and the Ecuadorian people. Although the specific details of her service were not clear, she knew that Ecuador was the place she had been searching for.

While Dr. Weaver was serving in Shell, a tragic event occurred that had a major impact on her future. During a visit to Shell, one of Dr. Weaver's sisters suffered a brain hemorrhage and had to be flown to Quito for emergency medical treatment. In Quito, a missionary nurse who had already arranged for immediate treatment, met Dr. Weaver's sister. This nurse knew little about Dr. Weaver, and nothing about her sister. Yet, she personally guaranteed payment of the hospital charges so Dr. Weaver's sister could receive the care she needed. Without this guarantee, it would have been impossible for Dr. Weaver's sister to receive medical care. (As is the case in many Third

World Countries, medical treatment in Ecuador is only available to those who can afford to pay for it)

The missionary nurse who met Dr. Weaver's sister was Sheila Leach, who was the Director of Community Development for HCJB World Radio. She visited Dr. Weaver's sister several times each day, bringing flowers, smuggling in hamburgers, and doing whatever else she could to provide comfort. When Dr. Weaver was able to travel to Quito, Ms. Leach made room for her to stay in her apartment. She was a modern-day Good Samaritan in every sense of the word.

Through this tragic situation, the paths of Dr. Weaver and Sheila Leach crossed. Out of difficulty came a blessing. A strong friendship developed between the two women. With 20 years of missionary experience, Ms. Leach was able to offer valuable insight and encouragement to Dr. Weaver as she considered missionary involvement in Ecuador.

After completing seven months of service at the hospital in Shell, Ecuador, Dr. Weaver returned to Fort Wayne where she worked for two years as a general surgeon with Indiana Surgical Specialists. During this short time Dr. Weaver built a successful practice and became a well-respected surgeon. She continued to have a desire to serve in Ecuador, and used her vacation time to return three times on short-term trips.

Upon completing her contract with Indiana Surgical Specialists, Dr. Weaver made plans to return to Ecuador on a permanent basis. In September 2001, she moved to Quito as a career missionary affiliated with HCJB World Radio. Dr. Weaver currently works in the Department of Public Development as a general surgeon . She is also the Director of the HCJB Clinic in San Lorenzo, Ecuador. San Lorenzo is located eight miles from the Columbian border and can be a very dangerous place. The people are desperately poor and would have no access to medical care were it not for the Clinic there. Dr. Weaver spends half her time in the San Lorenzo Clinic and the remainder of her time is spent performing surgery in HCJB clinics around Quito and in remote parts of Ecuador.

For information about Dr. Weaver and her work in Ecuador, please write to Latin-American Missions Board, PO Box 15663, Fort Wayne, IN 46885; or you may send an E-mail message to: info@LAMBonline.org.

This chapter was completed and ready to go to press when an event took place that so moved my heart, I felt the publication of the book needed to be brought to a halt. I felt it was necessary to include this in the chapter challenging all of us to "help those who are suffering and in need."

The world has been stunned as the news broadcast the horrible devastation in Sri Lanka. It has been encouraging to watch two former Presidents from opposing political parties, come together to appeal for the nation's help. Our world is blessed to have such organizations as the Red Cross and Feed the Children to intervene during times of human suffering.

We as individuals, communities and nations need to keep our hearts of compassion open to "help those who are suffering and in need."

℞

Seventeen

AVOID SEX UNTIL YOU ARE READY TO BECOME A PARENT.

Somewhere along the line of development we discover what we really are, and then we make our real decisions for which we are responsible. Make that decision primarily for yourself, because you can never really live anyone else's life... the influence you exert is through you own life and what you become yourself.

—Eleanor Roosevelt

Would you live with ease, do what you ought and not what you please.

—Benjamin Franklin

Responsibility is a thing people dread most of all. Yet it is the only thing in the world that develops us, gives us manhood and womanhood cyber.

—Frank Crane

The sad reality of our society today is that, despite some positive trends in our modern culture, the fact is that the absolute levels of most character-related problems remain higher than they were a few decades ago. To take the character and health of our next generation seriously, we need to take an honest look at the moral condition of our sexual culture.

We as Americans can applaud ourselves for the fact that there have been healthy changes as it relates to sexuality today as compared to that prior to the 1960s. In many homes, parents and kids are much more comfortable talking about sexual issues than a generation ago. Couples having sexual problems in marriage are far more comfortable seeking professional help and doing something about their frustrations. However, this greater openness in the sexuality of our popular culture today has been marked with many disturbing pitfalls.

The task of the family and school of teaching sexual self-control has been extremely difficult because young people are growing up in a world that constantly pushes sex. Bombarded by magazines like"Teen People" and television programs like "Beverly Hills 90210" our children are struggling to commit to moral and healthy choices that will leave them with fulfilled lives. "Facing Reality Sexually" is a curriculum created by James Coughlin. He comments, "We socialize kids to have sex. No culture in human history has ever done this to children."

The breakdown of our moral values as it relates to sex has spawned a devastating plague of challenges such as promiscuity, infidelity, fatherless children, unwed pregnancies, sexual addictions, sexually transmitted diseases, abortions, sexual harassment, sexual abuse of children, pornography that includes children, children acting out sexually—and the list could go on and on.

An interesting statistic has come out of Uganda, where a national policy of premarital abstinence and marital fidelity is enforced. It is the only country in the world succeeding in controlling the HIV/AIDS epidemic. In 1991 the percentage was 21% and in 2003 it was lowered to 6%. Now I'm not suggesting legislating morality, but I am declaring we must do more to teach responsibility for the purpose of character and health development . I am aware that this topic is delicate territory, laced with topical landmines, but this potential for controversy should not intimidate us if we truly care for our children. As unpopular as it may be, abstinence is recognized as the wisest choice for many reasons. Here are some reasons why we should not allow ourselves to be threatened to approach this subject:

- More than 1/2 million unmarried teens get pregnant each year.
- Having a baby is the surest route to poverty.
- One in three sexually active singles get a sexually transmitted disease by age 24.

- Prior to 1970, there were only two common STD's—Syphilis and Gonorrhea. Currently, there are more than twenty.
- 30% is the failure rate of condoms to prevent pregnancy for teens (the percentage can go higher because alcohol and drug abuse limits the ability to use condoms correctly, if at all).
- In the last twenty years, teens have had the largest increase in use of condoms. However, during this time, this same age group has had the greatest increase in sexually transmitted diseases.
- 2001 National Institute of Health responds that condoms provide NO PROVEN PROTECTION against six of the eight leading STDs.

An author that made an impression on me relating to this topic is Thomas Lickona in his previously mentioned book, *Character Matters.* Lickona points out that one way to prevent kids from being seduced into sexual activity is to make them aware of the factors that drew their peers into sexual involvement. Knowledge is truly power. Here are some of Lickona's insights:

1. **Sexual Attraction.** Human beings are sexual creatures; we are sexually interested and attracted to others. Sexual desire doesn't compel anyone to sex, but in the absence of inhibiting counter-influences it can easily lead to sexual activity.
2. **No good reason not to.** "I got sexually involved," says a senior, "because I couldn't answer the question—"Why shouldn't I have sex?"
3. **Partner pressure.** Pressure from a partner—a boyfriend or girlfriend they wanted to keep—is the reason teens most often cite for their initial decision to have sex.
4. **Desire to express love.** Many young people think sex is simply a natural way to express the love they feel for each other.
5. **Desire to be normal.** Says a high school health teacher, "In recent years, many kids have gotten it into their heads that there is something wrong with them if they don't have sexual intercourse by the time they are sixteen."

6. **Early dating.** A study in the "Journal of Adolescent Research" found that of those who began dating as seventh graders, 71% of boys and 90% of girls had intercourse by the time they graduated from high school. Of those who did not begin single dating until age sixteen, only 16% of boys and 18% of girls had sexual intercourse by high school graduation.
7. **Steady dating.** The same study found that steady dating, which typically increases the time a couple spends alone, significantly increase the likelihood of sexual intercourse.
8. **Need for intimacy.** Many young people, especially girls, turn to sex to try to meet the need for intimacy. "If Dad isn't there giving non-sexual attention," says one psychologist, "a girl will often go after sexual attention from boys."
9. **Low self-worth.** Says a girl who got pregnant at fifteen, "My brothers and their girlfriends said if you didn't do it you were a nerd. I had always been sort of an outcast, and I didn't want to be called a nerd."
10. **The search for identity.** Says Cheryl Jones, an adolescent therapist, "I see girls who, up until now, have been perfect kids— straight A's, followed all the rules—then they turn fifteen or sixteen and they think, " I don't want to be just what my parents want me to be." They know what they don't want to be, but they don't know what to be; so they become the opposite, a kind of anti-personality." (Becoming one's own person as a teenager is less likely to involve this kind of rebellion if parents, from childhood on, have been helping their children to define their own interests and sense of self.)
11. **Change in environment.** For some young people. sexuality starts when they enter a new environment such as college, where there is the potential to live more freely.
12. **Parental permissiveness.** Fourteen year old Courtney complained that her parents "Let me go over to my boyfriend's house when they know his parents aren't at home. That is weird." Eventually she and her boyfriend had sex.
13. **Parents' example.** Says a high school boy who lives with his divorced father, "What's the big deal about sex? A lot of my Dad's girlfriends spend the night."

14. **Nothing better to do.** In South Bronx, New York, where the teen pregnancy rate is nearly twice the national norm, a community agency sponsored an essay contest for adolescents on the question, "How Can the Problem of Teenage Pregnancy Be Solved?" One of the winning essays maintains that teens have sex, "because they are bored—they have nothing better to do". One pregnancy prevention program found that when teens got involved in community service, the pregnancy rate dropped.
15. **Sex education that doesn't send a clear abstinence message.** Says a boy in Los Angeles, "They pass out condoms, teach pregnancy–this and STD–that, but they never really say its wrong."
16. **Sexual abuse.** One in four girls and one in six boys are sexually abused by age eighteen. Sexually abused youth, often because of their low self-worth, are more likely to become sexually active, often with older partners.
17. **Drugs and alcohol.** Drugs and alcohol impair moral judgement and weaken inhibitions. Teens who say they have used drugs or have been drunk in the past month, for example, are much more likely to have had sex than teens who have never been drunk or used drugs.
18. **A highly sexualized environment.** A sexually stimulating media culture sends the unrelenting message that sex is the center of the universe. Add this to the sexualized peer environment created by young people themselves, including increasingly provocative dress.

It remains unclear as to whether there will come a voice from the nation crying out that we must do what is truly needed to build a more decent, healthy society. While the "jury is out" on this verdict, we must commit ourselves to the worthwhile endeavors of character and healthcare education. These moral erosions have not taken place as a result of a rapid overwhelming flood, but a slow and steady decline in our families, schools, and communities. Just as it has taken a process of time to happen, it will require time and effort to rebuild after this devastation. But it can be reversed if efforts become widespread, beginning with each individual. We can clean the air of a sexually toxic environment if we work together.

℞

Eighteen

EXPECT TO MAKE YOUR OWN WAY IN LIFE.

Ask not what your country can do for you,
but what you can do for your country.
—John F. Kennedy

I long to accomplish a great and noble task, but it is my chief duty
to accomplish small tasks as if they were great and noble.
—Helen Keller

There is no growth except in the fulfillment of obligation.
—Antonie de Saint-Exupeury

Without duty, life is soft and boneless; it cannot hold itself together.
—Joseph Joubert

Life without duties is obscene.
—Ralph Waldo Emerson

We cannot hope to scale moral heights by ignoring petty obligations.
—Agnes Repplier

My wife, Rhonda has a favorite quote from George Eliot that says, "It is never too late to be what you might have been." I, too, have come to appreciate the depth of the meaning to these words. In this present culture far too many people are not "making their own way in life" because of two adversaries to this Prescription. The first is an attitude of "entitlement," that tells a lie to the individual bearing this attitude. This lie says to them that they should not have to make their own way because others are responsible for their needs in life. What a horrible thief this is because it robs those who allow this thinking process from becoming "what they might have been."

The other attitude that will prevent someone from "making their own way in life" is the tendency to "blame." Blaming others for causing you to not become what you might have been will only result in a tragically wasted life. The words from the quote, "It's never too late to be what you might have been," becomes a great challenge to confront these obstacles and motivate all of us to make the choice to have the expectation of "making our own way in life."

I love and admire my wife, Rhonda. She has made this quote a living testimonial. Rhonda made a commitment to continue her education and to prepare herself to be able to "make her own way in life." The spring of 2005 brought great joy as I watched Rhonda march across the stage to receive her diploma for her Bachelor's Degree. It was such a rewarding commencement ceremony.

A part of my daily reading is the Investor's Business Daily. I believe the "IBD's 10 Secrets To Success" would be a valuable contribution to anyone desirous of "making their own way in life." Read them carefully and take a personal inventory of which traits are lacking or need improvement in your life.

1. **How you think is everything.** Always be positive. Think success, not failure. Beware of a negative environment.

2. **Decide upon your true dreams and goals.** Write down your specific goals and develop a plan to reach them.

3. **Take action.** Goals are nothing without action. Don't be afraid to get started. Just do it.

4. **Never stop learning.** Go back to school or read books. Get training and acquire skills.

5 **Be persistent and work hard.** Success is a marathon, not a sprint. Never give up.

6. **Learn to analyze details.** Get all the facts, all the input. Learn from your mistakes.

7. **Focus your time and money.** Don't let other people or things distract you.

8. **Don't be afraid to innovate; be different.** Following the herd is a sure way to mediocrity.

9. **Deal and communicate with people effectively.** No person is an island. Learn to understand and motivate others.

10. **Be honest and dependable; take responsibility.** Otherwise, numbers 1-9 won't matter.

All of us who are parents should know the difficulty of wanting to make a better life possible for our children than the life we had growing up. I well remember growing up the child of German immigrant parents. As I reflect on my childhood, and growing up in the city, I recall how we lived in the same building as our family-operated grocery store and delicatessen. My bedroom was in the basement, the first floor was the store, and the upstairs was where my parents slept. My father always wanted me to work in the grocery store with him, but my mother wanted me to be a doctor. What a blessing she was to me. From my birth she put away what little amounts of cash she could to save for my education. Life was not easy for us. My parents were honest and hard-working, putting in long hours at the store.

During those years I knew I wanted to make life easier and better for my family. I often wonder if this principle of wanting to provide more for the next generation has somehow robbed them of their potential for making their own way in life. Maybe "handing them life on a silver platter" is a detriment, not an advantage. I feel strongly that this prescription will do much to build strong character and bring more peace in our communities.

While perusing Border's Book Store, I came across a title that caught my attention. The book was entitled *Uncle Sam's Plantation*, written by an amazing lady name Star Parker. I purchased the book and my heart was stirred to the extent that I brought her to Fort Wayne as a guest lecturer. During her stay in my hometown she addressed the Annual Banquet of the NAACP, spoke in several high school assemblies, and conducted TV and radio interviews. Her challenging message is her own testimony of rising above potentially overwhelming circumstances.

Star had no education and no skills—a single mother with a drug dependency, engulfed in a life of prostitution and cheating the Welfare System just to survive. Star made a commitment that she was going to "Live the Good Life," and pursued the positive avenues that would lead her our of her desperation into a new life of "making her own way."

All of us who were fortunate enough to hear Star's story of success were moved emotionally, and came to the realization that when an individual expects to "make their own way in life" they can transform, not only their families, but their communities also.

If every individual takes the Eighteenth Prescription to heart, there will be less crime. I believe there will be less of a compulsion for corporate and street crime. I conclude that we will be more at peace with ourselves and those around us as a result of fulfilling our own unique duties and accepting the responsibilities of our own destinies. This will contribute to building stronger relationships through this self-reliance. I savor the Irish Proverb that says," You got to do your own growing up no matter how tall your grandfather was." If each of us will measure up to what our potential is, the anger and frustration will diminish in each of our lives.

I am sure by now that in reading this book you know that I enjoy reading. I especially relish quoting the various sources I have used throughout this book—they have made an impact on my life. The Latin Proverb says, "If there is no wind, row." If we take this Prescription to "make our own way in life," we must not depend on outside forces to make our way for us. That's why this proverb is of notable interest to me. Along with expecting other sources to contribute to our making our way, another hindrance to our sense of duty is that of arranging our priorities properly. Joseph Quinci said, "When you have a number of disagreeable duties to perform, always do the most disagreeable first." I have found in my acquaintances that those who are successful in their professional lives have disciplines of "making their own way in life" that apply to every area of their personal lives as well.

Those who are successful in their professional lives most generally have discipline in every area of their life that perhaps are disagreeable in carrying out. Many of us do not enjoy mowing our lawns, making our beds, keeping our desks clean, washing the dishes and carrying out the garbage. It is easy to allow our garages to fall into disarray. The discipline in small areas is what determines the character for the large things we would like to accomplish.

There is an author who has influenced all who have read his material. I, too, have gleaned many insights from M. Scott Peck. One book in particular is *The Road Less Traveled.* Dr. Peck's opening statement in the book is, "Life is difficult." Dr. Peck makes it clear that most of our problems emotionally comes as a result of either not believing this is true, or not being willing to accept the truthfulness of this statement. When we believe either one of these two things we will not "make our own way in life." Peck goes on to say that the joy of life is never derived without difficulty. Fulfillment, according to Dr. Peck, is found in confronting and working through the difficulties that arise throughout our lifetime.

Build upon the premise Dr. Peck expounds throughout the structure of his book. In order for us all to be able to work through these difficulties of life, Dr. Peck explains, we need four essential tools. I will briefly introduce these four tools, but I encourage you, as a reader, to acquire a copy of his book so you can read the wonderfully detailed description of each of these four points.

In Dr. Peck's attempt to equip us to travel the road less taken, one of the tools he provides is "a dedication to truth." Unquestionably truthfulness is always the best means of dealing with difficulties in helping us "make our own way in life." As we have been taught, "Honesty is the best policy."

The second vital tool to making our own way is that of "delayed gratification." All of us know the struggle of wanting what we want when we want it. I have a friend who often says to me, "The greatest problem with immediate gratification is that it just is not quick enough!" Many of us have witnessed those who never make their own way in life because they decide on the satisfaction of the moment rather than the discipline of delaying for a greater fulfillment that can be achieved later. Many people's education has been wasted; many opportunities have been forfeited because of choosing not to delay their own gratification.

The third tool Dr. Peck believes is important to our facing life's difficulties is that of "accepting responsibility." In *The Road Less Traveled*, Peck makes so clear the importance of differentiating between being responsible for people, and being responsible to people. As we learn the distinction of these two concepts we are freed to "make our own way in life."

The fourth tool of our character development is that of "staying balanced." I am convinced, along with Dr. Peck, that each time my difficulties have become compounded, I have not practiced staying balanced. I remember a patient who wasted many days of anxiety about a medical procedure because he was unaware of what would be involved. The fear of the unknown will always cause us to lose our balance. Three days were spent without eating or sleeping. Fear plagued my patient. When I came to the hospital room the patient was amazed, as in a matter of only a few seconds, I expedited the procedure, and all the anxiety was for naught. As I talked with the patient over the years, we enjoyed laughing together over the event. He has shared with me often of the great lesson he learned about the importance of staying balanced because that which we fear never turns out to be actually what we think it will be.

We can't stay balanced by just looking at the challenges that prepare us the very best for "making our own way in life." If we only look we will lose our emotional equilibrium, and never complete those challenges. I trust that all, no matter what stage in life, who are contemplating making a commitment to "make their own way in life," will consider Dr. Peck's book an integral part of their personal inventory of resources.

Our main business is not to see what lies dimly at a distance,
but to do what life clearly has at hand.

—Thomas Carlyle

When you work you are a flute through whose heart the
whispering of the hours turns to music. To love life through
labor is to be intimate with life's inmost secret. All work is
empty save when there is love, for work is love made visible.

—Kahlil Gobran

Nineteen

PRACTICE CHARITY— BEING WILLING TO FORGIVE YOURSELF AND OTHERS.

Bitterness is like drinking poison, hoping it will kill the other person.
—Unknown

Love is that condition in which the happiness of another person is essential to your own.
—Robert A. Heinlein

Who so loves believes the impossible.
—Elizabeth Barrett Browning

People need loving the most when they deserve it the least.
—Mary Crowley

A wise man will make haste to forgive because he knows the true value of time, and will not suffer it to pass away in unnecessary pain.
—Samuel Johnson

If you haven't forgiven yourself something, how can you forgive others?
—Delores Huerta

Don't carry a grudge. While you're carrying the grudge, the other guy's out dancing.
—Buddy Hackett

If life is going to be free from our basic and primitive instincts of revenge and our first impulse to get even we must live with a spirit of mercy. I believe that mercy and compassion always join together as manifestations of authentic charity. Compassion must first be intended to yourself. When you judge yourself harshly for mistakes and failing to follow some standard, you are refusing to accept your humanness. Give yourself mercy, and authentic compassion; for it is then you will be able to give it to another.

It is amazing, being a part of a bilingual background, how the English language is so limited in its vocabulary. A prime example is the word "love." We use the word love to describe how we feel about a hot fudge sundae, our pet dog, our children, our work and our life-long mate. I don't believe any of us intend that the word "love" have the same application in all these examples. That is why there was a book written by a man named C. S. Lewis that had a great influence on my understanding of the word "love."

C. S. Lewis authored *The Chronicles of Narnia*, and also a little-known book entitled *The Four Loves.* The first of the four words he describes is *eros*, from which the English word "erotic" is derived. It is sad that this word, through iniquity, has come to be identified with the dark side of human personality. The original intention and usage of the word was to describe one's physical attraction toward another individual. Unquestionably, eros as originally defined, would have a vital significance at the beginning of a relationship. Those who are not initially attracted to another person have never known the joy of the "falling in love" experience. The problems that come as a result of only having this level of love is that as we grow older and grow up, through experience, we learn that physical attraction is not enough to sustain a relationship for very long.

The second word C. S. Lewis used that is translated from the Greek into English as love is *storge*, the word used in Greek culture to describe one's love for his family. We have already, in previous prescriptions, shared our convictions about the importance of love, honor, and respect for our families. In an age where we live seeing the home and families fractured by divorce, and the slow erosion of the family unit due to the demands of time, family love is slowly eluding our society. It also saddens me, as I shared earlier in this book, to see so many who have no way of relating to family because of abuse and negligence in their formative years within their home environment.

However, even those who have had the privilege and blessing of being raised in a nuclear family unit where love was freely shared and openly demonstrated, there still comes a time that family love, by necessity, will be altered. Each young man and woman, raised as a son or daughter with happy interactions, comes to a point in life when they meet that special someone, and leave their family relationship to embark on a journey of establishing a new family unit of their own. Because of this, C. S. Lewis points out, there must be more definition for our understanding of love.

The third word that Lewis defines as love is the Greek word *philea.* Philea is a word that, when we pause to think about it, has several English words that can aid our understanding. The name of the city Philadelphia came form the combination of two Greek words meaning "city" and "brotherly love." Those familiar with horticulture are aware of the plant philodendron. The philodendron is named from this Greek word because of its heart-shaped leaf. Philea is the word that gives meaning to love as expressed by our emotions, and feelings and passions of life. So, of course, this is a great word to communicate our affections, and a great foundation in building relationships. But as we all know, our feelings can be hurt and our hearts, often times, are wounded; and our tendency is to withdraw and isolate. An often-repeated statement that has always grieved me—"Hurt me once, shame on you; hurt me twice, shame on me." Certainly, self-preservation is a driving force, and when our feelings have been trampled on we tend to not want to love again. I would like to quote from Mr. Lewis' book, *The Four Loves,* where he paraphrases St. Augustine:

> *To love at all is to be vulnerable. Love anything, and your heart will certainly be rung and broken. If you want to make sure of keeping it intact, you must give your heart to no one, not even an animal. Wrap it carefully round hobbies and little luxuries; avoid all entanglements; lock it up in the safe casket or coffin of your selfishness. But in that casket—safe and dark, motionless, barren—it will change. It will not be broken; it will become unbreakable, impenetrable, irredeemable...The only place outside heaven you can be perfectly safe from all dangers of love is hell.*

These are truly stirring words that motivate us to find a deeper meaning of love!

That is why Mr. Lewis introduces us to the fourth concept of love. The Greek word *agape* is the word that he challenges every individual to achieve. Just as *philea* is the love of emotion and affection, *agape* love is love of the intellect based on choices, and is directly related to the mind and the exercising of the will. Others have defined this love as "an unselfish choice for another's highest good." This is the love that will help us when physical attraction may not be present. When not surrounded by the support of family, and our affections and emotions have been drained, we still have within us, the resources to make a choice to make a difference. This love, rather than offering the shallow warm fuzzies, is a love that puts teeth into life.

As Prescription Nineteen seeks to convey, one of the greatest expressions of love is through the act of forgiveness. I believe forgiveness is one of the most radical concepts in human interaction. Nothing will further our mission statement "to promote peace and build character" like the act of forgiveness.

I would like to offer six aspects of forgiveness. I have learned to differ forgiveness from pardon. Forgiveness involves the individual's emotional response toward the one who has offended them. Pardon deals with the consequences of the offense. A wife who has been battered, or a child who has been molested or abused, in order to have a healthy future, must learn to separate these two words. If bitterness and resentment are harbored in these people's hearts, they will be the prisoners. If they can come to the place of forgiveness, it does not mean they should feel responsible to remove the consequences of the offense of the person who inflicted their pain. Sometimes the consequences will reveal how sincere the other individual is in wanting to restore relationship.

Abuse, as we shared earlier, should never go unnoticed nor unreported. If the offense has broken the law, the consequences must be handled by the legal system.

The first of the six aspects is: forgiveness involves maintaining a positive attitude toward the offense rather than a negative attitude toward the offender.

Seeking professional help can aid the offended person in extracting the significance of his or her own personal development from the offense. I don't believe we are able, on our own volition, to achieve that understanding, but through patience and through seeking help, I am convinced these insights can be accomplished.

The second aspect shows us that forgiveness can help us view the offender as an instrument to make one stronger. The third, forgiveness can allow you to look at the wounds of your offense as a way of drawing attention to the offender's needs. That is why having the courage to report abuse to the proper authorities may put the individual who has offended in a position where they can receive the necessary help they need.

Fourth, forgiveness recognizes that bitterness is only self-destructive. When we are bitter it will not only be directed toward the offender, but a bitter heart is the heart through which you will perceive and relate to all other individuals.

Fifth, forgiveness realizes the offended is already receiving the consequences of their offense to you. Let me explain how I have come to understand this fifth concept of forgiveness. Perhaps the person who wounded you is disrespectful and irresponsible, and was totally unconscious, due to the lack of caring, of your life and the pain they have brought. Through hurting you, they have become hardened in their own hearts. There are others who, now they seek to have relationships with, but because of that hardness, they have rendered themselves incapable of intimacy, and thus, they are destined to live a shallow self-centered life.

Sixth, forgiveness will always carry with us a willingness to cooperate in the healing of the offender's life, if they have gone through the necessary processes of confronting, and maturely dealing with the consequences of their forgiveness.

I have found a wonderful quote whose author is anonymous, but its truth is eternal:

When forgiveness denies there is anger,
Acts as if it never happened,
Smiles as though it never hurt,
Fakes as though it is all forgotten...
Do not offer it,
Do not trust it,
Do not depend on it,
It is not forgiveness,
It is a magical fantasy.

It is my hope that these truths of love and forgiveness will be a

Prescription that will bring help to soul and spirit. Remember, forgiveness must begin with you. You cannot give away what you do not have, and that is forgiveness, but you cannot keep what you do not give away, and that is your "unselfish choice for other's highest good."

As I shared in Chapter 11, on the Prescription regarding "support peace," it was my honor to be a speaker in the"Circle of Hope: A Healing Memorial to September 11." It was conducted on the beautiful campus of Gulf Coast University, near Naples, Florida. One of the handouts read as part of the memorial service was entitled, "The Twelve Rules in Love." They made a great impression on me, and I would like to close this chapter by simply listing the beautiful "Rules In Love:"

1. Thou shalt avoid avarice like the deadly pestilence, and embrace its opposite.

2. Thou shalt keep thyself chaste for the sake of her whom thou lovest.

3. Thou shalt not knowingly strive to break up a correct love affair that someone else is engaged in.

4. Thou shalt not choose for thy love anyone whom a natural sense of forbids thee to marry.

5. Be mindful completely to avoid falsehood.

6. Thou shalt not have many that know thy love affair.

7. Being obedient in all things to commands of ladies, thou shalt ever strive to ally thyself to the service of love.

8. In giving and receiving love's solaces, let modesty be ever present.

9. Thou shalt speak no evil.

10. Thou shalt not be a revealer of love affairs.

11. Thou shalt be in all things polite and courteous.

12 In practicing the solaces of love thou shalt not exceed the desires of thy lover.

℞

Twenty

RESPECT THE ENVIRONMENT.

Now God gave Solomon wisdom and very great discernment and breadth of mind, like the sand that is on the seashore....and his fame was known in all the surrounding nations. He also spoke 3,000 proverbs and his songs were 1,005. And he spoke of trees, from the cedars of Lebanon, even to the hyssop that grows upon the wall; he spoke also of animals and birds and creeping things and fish. And men came from all the peoples to hear the wisdom of Solomon from all the kings of the earth who had heard of his wisdom.

—I Kings 4:29-34 (NAS)

I found these words of the Old Testament describing King Solomon to be especially interesting as an insight to his great success. For those who travel to Israel, it is astounding to see the archeological finds of the tremendous architectural achievements of this great king. One of the " Seven Wonders of the World," Solomon's Temple, is a great historical monument to this man's abilities.

With that as his legacy, he was also able to spend such quality time taking in the beauty of his environment and the wonderful creatures of nature. The magnificence of his surroundings became the inspiration for his poetry and songs that remain with us, even to the present day.

Recently I returned to New York City for a special occasion. My wife, Rhonda, and I were pleased to be part of my 50th high school reunion at Concordia High School in Bronxville, New York. It was hard to believe that fifty years had passed since my high school graduation. One memory that stands out in my mind is choosing a college to attend after my high school graduation. I was fortunate enough to get grades that made it possible for me to choose from a wide-range of universities across the United States. My decision included, first and foremost, my desire to become a doctor. (I think my mother whispered that in my ear on the day I was born!) I sent for a number of brochures, but the one that struck me the most was from Indiana University in Bloomington, Indiana. I still remember looking at the promotional material. On the cover were pictures of a beautiful tree-covered campus. I knew I wanted to go to school in such a splendid, scenic environment, and I applied there, and spent the next nine years on that lovely campus.

Respect for the environment has been a part of my entire life. I have no greater pleasure and source of relaxation than to rise early in the morning when at our lake cottage, and walk around the shoreline, taking in all of nature and enjoying the lovely trees, shrubs and flowers. I love watching the hummingbirds, seemingly frozen in air, sipping the nectar of my honeysuckle. The beauty surrounding me seems to awaken a connection to life for me. I plant trees and flowers regularly to further appreciate nature's creation. It is a time of renewal every year, and even now, in the month of December, I am looking forward, already, to spring to see how my plants have fared the winter.

It was especially exciting one year for me to bring the Community Performing Arts Choir, a choir of fifty young people from the inner city of my hometown of Fort Wayne, Indiana, to our cottage for the day. We played, swam, took boat rides, and at the end of the day, had a concert. I think it was most probably the first time those children had ever been to a lake. I shall never forget the good time we all had. I knew they shared my respect for the environment as I observed them picking up pop cans and making sure that there was no debris left on the grounds that would reflect disrespect for what they experienced that day.

I recall, as a boy, listening to the commentators on Arbor Day. I appreciate the efforts of the Arbor Day Foundation to preserve our trees. I encourage you to visit their web site and look over their promotional material. I think we must be aware that it is important to plant trees and preserve our forests. I remember planting a tree in front of the Men's Quad at Indiana University while I was in school there.

When I returned to the campus for my 40th Class Reunion I was pleased to see that the tree had grown into a beautiful Oak. The preservation of nature in a reasonable manner is the principle of the "Call of Life." It is in appreciation and participation with nature that our life forces, quantum energies, positive vibrations and mental balance are restored.

I encourage you to make a practice of walking through parks or woods, or wherever nature is closest to you. Listen to the wind, the rustling of the leaves, the songs of the birds, and you will feel a direct connection to your sense of well-being. Look up at the stars and planets. Take an interest in the grandeur of the universe. When you contemplate the majesty and harmony of the universe, it makes the troubles and chaos of our world seem petty and small. Einstein made a very fitting comment along this line. He said," I can believe in a God that created the harmony of the universe." I savor the rain, the snow, the dew, the wind, the birds and animals. Incorporate this appreciation of nature into your life and you will bask in the wonder, the beauty and inspiration of it all. Lead a life in harmony with the universe and the environment and you will experience the "Call of Life."

Environmentalists should not be the title of an elite group of people pushing a political platform. We should all consider ourselves environmentalists by showing concern for the space closest to us at any given moment in life. At home, at school, at work, and even where we recreate. Isn't it interesting that "recreate" is the joining of two words, "re" and "create." When we play golf or tennis, swim or fish or whatever we do for relaxation, we are "re-creating" ourselves by escaping from our daily pressures for a time. I would like to suggest that we can "re-create" our environment as part of our recreation by not leaving any trash and helping to pick up debris left on the courts, beach, or in the library. We need to make it our duty to help keep the environment clean.

This reminds me of an incident that happened to me when my daughter was playing at NYU. I sat in Washington Park, enjoying the sunshine one day while waiting for her. The park is about the size of a city block. There were three policemen standing around the park and countless people sitting on the benches enjoying the day. I was appalled that though here were plenty of trash cans throughout the park there was a tremendous amount of garbage everywhere. With nothing else to do while waiting on my daughter, I went around the whole park and picked up all the garbage and placed it in four of the large trash cans. Nothing was said while I did my "clean-up," but I certainly hope that those in the park who were watching me got the message—that a clean environment is the responsibility of *all* of us.

We have so many areas to include when we talk about environments. Too often we think only of the great outdoors, and that certainly must be a major concern for all of us. However, I think we also have to think of noise pollution, such as the use of cell phones when you are in close proximity to others. It is a discourtesy to force other to listen to your private conversations. Cell phones should be turned off in certain places such as churches or restaurants unless one is part of an emergency response such as physicians, firemen, etc. And even for them, their phones can be put on"vibrate." This form of pollution has become a serious problem in our culture today and we must do our part to keep noise at a minimum. If neighbors live close by, as in an apartment complex or trailer park or housing addition one should be courteous enough to keep the decibels down on our stereos and TVs.

There are other areas in which we can show respect for our environment. For example, every member of a family can respect the home environment in simple ways. Keeping their rooms clean, taking out the trash, picking up trash left in the yard. Regulating the volume of music not only shows respect for the home environment, but also treats others as you would like to be treated.

I mentioned previously in this book that if your are a smoker, you should do your best to quit; it is dangerous to your health. However, if you choose to smoke, you should do so in an area where other people are not exposed to the secondary smoke. Not only is the smoke offensive to the environment, but dangerous to the health of those around you.

One day as I went to observe the wheelchair basketball team practice (I was privileged to be able to address them after practice), I noted the title "Turnstone" with a beautiful bird identified as the logo for this organization. I asked one of the administrators how the Turnstone bird came to represent this agency and here is the quote that I received:

> *The Turnstone bird symbolizes the spirit of the agency by its relentless adapting of many body parts to move heavy stones to find food. Also, when an object is too heavy for one Turnstone to move alone, other Turnstone birds gather to assist. Children and adults at Turnstone learn to overcome their disabilities by adapting their bodies to perform functions most people take for granted. When the disability is difficult to overcome, other people such as you gather to assist. The mental image of a bird in flight creates a feeling of what Turnstone strives for—helping individuals with disabilities gain freedom and attain new heights of personal growth and increased independence.*

Perhaps if all of us spent a little more time "respecting the environment" we could gain, like King Solomon of old, inspiring illustrations from the world around us.

I have often referred in this book to Dr. Wayne Dyer's works and I would like to close this final chapter with some suggestions that have come to me by way of inspiration from reading and listening to Dr. Dyer:

1. Make a gift to yourself by allocating some time each week to immerse yourself in nature. Wilderness is therapeutic. Make an appointment to observe the perfection of the natural world.

2. Write your reactions to your nature experience in poetry or in essay. Don't be threatened that you are not a poet, just bare your feelings as you communed with nature.

3. On your next family vacation consider including in your itinerary a mountain hike, a canoe ride down a river, or camping out under the stars. These experiences will make for a life-time of memories. Sometime, sleep outdoors in your own backyard, or just do something that will allow nature to play a more dominant and enthusiastic role in your life.

20 PRESCRIPTIONS FOR LIVING THE GOOD LIFE

1. Treat others as you would like to be treated.
2. Be honest; do not lie, cheat or steal—make your word your bond.
3. Treat life with care; avoid risky behavior.
4. Practice showing respect for authority; parents, teachers, police, and government.
5. Do not let physical or mental abuse go unnoticed.
6. Read a book—regularly.
7. Be tolerant of others beliefs.
8. Express honor, love, and respect for your family.
9. Make a commitment to continue education throughout your life.
10. Show respect for all life, human and animals.
11. Avoid violence, practice non-violence, support peace.
12. Celebrate our differences: sex, race, background, appearance, and disabilities.
13. Seek knowledge, wisdom, good character, and pursue excellence.
14. Practice health—control: exercise your body and mind.
15. Do not abuse your body-avoid tobacco, alcohol, and drugs.
16. Help those who are suffering or in need.
17. Avoid sex until you are ready to become a parent.
18. Expect to make your own way in life.
19. Practice charity—being willing to forgive yourself and others.
20. Respect the environment.

THE CALL OF LIFE

Treat others as you'd like
to be treated
Peace on Earth will live on

Be honest and truthful
Do not steal
Make your word your bond

Treat life with care
Avoid risky behavior
If you do you'll find favor

Respect authority
When others rage
honor your teachers, the
government, the brave

When the broken wonder if their
tears are wasted cries
Be their ears, be their eyes

Chorus:
Life needs you, life needs me
All our hopes, all our dreams
For inside us all is the call of life

Read books often
Light the dark
And learn what's in your heart
Be open
To what others believe
And learn what's in your heart

Honor your family
The place you call home
Love, thirst for knowledge keeps
hope alive

Make commitment
Be a learner for life
This thirst for knowledge keeps
hope alive

Respect all life
Man and creature small or great
Destiny will guide your fate

Chorus:
Life needs you, life needs me
All our hopes, all our dreams
These soul prescriptions
Will open doors through time
Cause a gift to shine
Keep the will alive
And give us faith to follow
the call of life

Avoid violence
Fill the streets with peace
Complete the dream of Dr. King

Celebrate our differences
Every face, every race
You'll see we're equal through
eyes of grace

Let good character
Guard your name
Let excellence seal your quest for
fame

Train mind and body
Practice health control
And clarity will fill your soul

Avoid those habits
Destined to destroy
Let discipline give birth to joy

Chorus:
Life needs you, life needs me
All our hopes, all our dreams
For inside of us all is the call of life

Touch the suffering
heal their pain
One day you'll reap the same

If you will wait
Till you say 'I do"
True love will find you

Face your mountains
Tell your doubt "I believe"
And forge a path to your dream

Forgive yourself and others
When there's no reason to
Prison doors will open inside you

If we respect the earth, the sky,
the sea
We'll give mother nature her
legacy

Chorus:
Life needs you, life needs me
All our hopes, all our dreams
These soul prescriptions
Will open doors through time
Cause a gift to shine
Keep the will alive
And give us faith to follow
the call of life